The Quran
Essential Teachings

Abdur Raheem Kidwai

JAICO PUBLISHING HOUSE

Ahmedabad Bangalore Chennai
Delhi Hyderabad Kolkata Mumbai

Published by Jaico Publishing House
A-2 Jash Chambers, 7-A Sir Phirozshah Mehta Road
Fort, Mumbai - 400 001
jaicopub@jaicobooks.com
www.jaicobooks.com

Published in arrangement with
The Islamic Foundation
Markfield Conference Centre
Ratby Lane, Markfield
Leicestershire, LE67 9SY, United Kingdom

To be sold only in India, Bangladesh, Bhutan,
Pakistan, Nepal, Sri Lanka and the Maldives.

THE QURAN: ESSENTIAL TEACHINGS
ISBN 81-7992-569-2

First Jaico Impression: 2006
Fourth Jaico Impression: 2010

Printed by
Repro India Limited, Mumbai

Contents

Preface

The Qur'ān occupies the pride of place in the lives of Muslims. Being Allah's final and perfect guidance it instructs Muslims in each and every aspect of their personal and public life. Furthermore, the Qur'ān exhorts Muslims to study it and reflect on its meaning and message, which is bound to enlighten and develop them. However, for millions of English-speaking Muslims, some English translations and a few introductory books on the Qur'ān are the only resource for gaining the knowledge of the Qur'ān and deriving Allah's guidance for their self-development. Generally speaking, the material available in English on the Qur'ān fails to meet these objectives adequately. The English translations of the Qur'ān are addressed mostly to specialized readers, and presuppose some background knowledge on the part of readers of comparative religion, theology, history and Qur'ānic terminology. Those not so equipped tend to be rather put off by the copious, scholarly notes explicating doctrinal, linguistic, legal and historical allusions of the Qur'an.

Another shortcoming in most of the books on the Qur'ān in English is the authors' predilection for using freely and frequently Arabic/Qur'ānic terms. The readers not familiar with such terms hazard guesswork which is not acceptable in this serious study.

The present work is addressed to the English-speaking reading public interested in grasping the meaning and message of the Qur'ān. In pursuance of this aim, some basic Qur'ānic terms, concepts and themes are explained in a simple language. The work is intended to help readers get an idea of the Qur'ānic worldview – the articles of faith, particularly the concepts of God, Messengership and the Hereafter. Needless to add, these beliefs lie at the core of Islamic faith and practices. For a better appreciation of the concept of God in Islam, it is followed by discussion on the Unseen, Creation and mankind. This should bring into sharper relief the role of God in the universe, and more importantly, God-man relationship in Islam. Religious duties in Islam – Prayer, Fasting, *Zakāh* and *Ḥajj* are elucidated mainly in terms of their rationale, and their all-pervading impact on man's personal and collective life. This, in turn, throws light on the Qur'ānic value system which is elaborated further by spelling out the traits of believers in the Qur'ān, hallmarks of the Straight Way prescribed by the Qur'ān and the Qur'ānic code of conduct governing social relations. The last section focuses on the Qur'ānic guidance related to treating family members in particular, and fellow human beings in general.

According to the Qur'ān, each and every human action should be permeated with God-consciousness. Therefore, the book concludes with the explanation of the Qur'ānic concept of supplication. According to the Qur'ān, supplication constitutes a direct link between Allah and man, enabling man to lead a God-oriented life.

This account of the message of the Qur'ān, with occasional comparison with major world faiths, should help readers form a clear idea of the Qur'ānic guidance on some major issues faced by them. It is hoped the present book will serve the needs of those new to the study of the Qur'ān. As an introductory work it should familiarize them with basic Qur'ānic terms and concepts which will help them grasp better advanced works on the Qur'ān. May Allah accept this humble effort in the cause of promoting a wider readership of the Qur'ān among English-speaking readers. May Allah pardon the author for any inadvertent lapse in construing and conveying the message of the Qur'ān.

October 2004 CE
Sha'bān 1425 H

Professor A.R. Kidwai
Aligarh Muslim University, INDIA
sulaim_05@yahoo.co.in

Foreword

The Qur'ān: Essential Teachings is intended to complement and supplement the Islamic Foundation's two earlier publications – (i) *The Qur'ān: Basic Teachings* by Khurshid Ahmad, T.B. Irving and M.M. Ahsan and (ii) *Way to the Qur'ān* by Khurram Murad. Like the above mentioned works, the present one too, seeks to prepare the reader mentally for embarking on a sustained, fruitful study of the Qur'ān.

Contained in the present work is a fairly elaborate explanation of twenty Qur'ānic terms and concepts with a view to highlighting the Qur'ānic viewpoint on some major issues of faith, religious obligations and social life. The author, associated for many years with the Foundation's projects on the Qur'ān, has drawn material from both classical and modern Qur'ānic scholarship. His main objective is to present before readers the Qur'ānic guidance in a simple jargon-free language. So doing, he refrains from indulging in any philosophical or juridical debate. It is earnestly hoped that the present work will be read with much profit by general readers and succeed in its aim of conveying effectively the message of the Qur'ān to those who are unable to study the Qur'ān in its Arabic original. May Allah Subḥānahū wa-Ta'ālā enable the Foundation to embark upon other useful projects for spreading far and wide the meaning and message of the Qur'ān.

I take this opportunity to thank Br. Abdur Rashid Siddiqi for his valuable suggestions and the Foundation production team, especially Br. Naiem Qaddoura and Br. Nasir Cadir. May Allah reward the author and the team in both the worlds.

Leicester, UK
1425 H/2004 CE

M. Manazir Ahsan
Director General

Transliteration Table

Consonants. Arabic

initial: unexpressed medial and final:

ء	'	د	d	ض	ḍ	ك	k
ب	b	ذ	dh	ط	ṭ	ل	l
ت	t	ر	r	ظ	ẓ	م	m
ث	th	ز	z	ع	'	ن	n
ج	j	س	s	غ	gh	هـ	h
ح	ḥ	ش	sh	ف	f	و	w
خ	kh	ص	ṣ	ق	q	ي	y

Vowels, diphthongs, etc.

Short:	ـَ a	ـِ i	ـُ u
long:	ـَا ā	ـِي ī	ـُو ū
diphthongs:		ـَوْ aw	
		ـَيْ ay	

1

Almighty Allah

Say: He is Allah, the One. Allah, the Unique. He does not give birth. Nor was He given birth to. There is no one equal to Him.

(al-Ikhlāṣ 112:1-4)

CENTRAL to the Islamic worldview is the concept of Allah. Throughout the Qur'ān His numerous features, creative power and perfect knowledge are described. In many *aḥādīth* too, the Prophet Muḥammad (peace and blessings be upon him) is seen throwing light on His attributes. The reference above from *Sūrah al-Ikhlāṣ* offers the quintessence of His unique being. Unlike other *sūrahs al-Ikhlāṣ* does not deal with any other theme or issue of this world or the Next. Rather, it focuses exclusively on Him. His first and foremost attribute is that He is the only true God. It thus does away with all false notions of polytheism. Equally significant is His uniqueness. There is nothing like Him. All human language fails to give an idea of His being. His uniqueness consists also in His attributes. All that He has accomplished and keeps on doing is simply beyond anyone's capacity or imagination. Many earlier communities, including the Hindus and Christians, had developed fallacious views about His being. The Qur'ān dismisses such erroneous views, asserting that in His nature, person and attributes, no one is equal to Him.

On studying the following passage one gets a better idea of some of His attributes, especially His all-embracing power and authority. The verse is therefore, known as "*Āyat al-Kursī*", the verse describing His throne:

Allah! There is no god besides He. He is the Ever-Living, Self-Subsisting and Eternal. Neither slumber nor sleep can ever seize Him. His is whatever is in the heavens and on earth. Who can intercede with Him, except with His permission? He knows whatever was before them and whatever shall be after them. And they do not encompass anything of His knowledge, except what He wills. His throne extends over the heavens and the earth. And He does not feel any fatigue in guarding and preserving them. For He is the Most High, the Supreme.

(al-Baqarah 2:255)

This verse vividly demonstrates His divine majesty and providence. Furthermore, one gets the distinct impression that He is the only force in the entire universe, which demolishes any notion of a plurality of gods. In the same vein is the emphasis placed on His eternality, without any beginning or end. He is not some Christ-God who faced crucifixion. Rather, He is Almighty, supporting all that exists. No one can boast of closeness with Him. Islam does not admit the concept of an intermediary who can recommend someone's case to Him. He is so perfect that He does not need any rest or sleep. This particular point assumes greater significance in that it refutes the Jewish and Christian idea of God "resting" on the seventh day after His exertion in creating the universe. (Genesis 2:2-3)

In keeping with its assertion that all the excellent names denoting perfection and unsurpassable glory belong only to Allah, the Qur'ān employs a host of names for Him, indicating as these do His varied and perfect attributes. The following passage, abounding in such names, brings to the fore some of His outstanding attributes.

He is Allah. There is no god besides He. He knows all things, both hidden and open. He is the Most Compassionate, Most Merciful.

He is Allah. There is no god other than Him. He is the Sovereign, the Holy, the source of peace and security, the Guardian of faith, the Protector, the Almighty, the Irresistible, the Supreme. Glory be to Allah. Exalted is He above the partners they attribute to Him. He is Allah, the Creator, the Maker, the Fashioner, His are the excellent names. Whatever is in the heavens and on earth glorifies His praise. He is Almighty, the Wise.

(al-Ḥashr 59:22-24)

Allah the Almighty, the All-Knowing. He forgives sins, accepts repentance, is severe in punishment and the Lord of power. There is no god but He. To Him is the final return.

(al-Ghāfir 40:2-3)

Whatever is in the heavens and on earth declares the praise and glory of Allah. He is Almighty, the Wise. To Him belongs the dominion of the heavens and the earth. It is He Who gives life and death and has power over all things. He is the first and the last, the manifest and the immanent. And He has full knowledge of everything.

(al-Ḥadīd 57:1-3)

Of His numerous attributes, those that are prominent include His absolute power and authority, His all-embracing knowledge, and total control over life and death. In recognition of these, all that exists in the universe praises and glorifies Him. Man, gifted with free-will, may choose to affirm or deny Him. However, man is blessed with intellect which guides him to believe in and serve Him. His knowledge and creative power are emphasised throughout the Qur'ān:

To Allah belongs all that is in the heavens and on earth. Whatever you reveal or conceal of what is in your minds, Allah will call you to account for it. He forgives whom He pleases, and punishes whom He pleases. For Allah has power over all things.

(al-Baqarah 2:284)

Some recurrent attributes of Allah in the Qur'ān which help man form a mental picture of Him are:

- *al-Raḥmān* (the Most-Compassionate)
- *al-Raḥīm* (the Most-Merciful)
- *al-Ḥakīm* (the Wise)
- *Rabb al-'Ālamīn* (the Lord of the worlds)
- *al-Khāliq* (the Creator)
- *al-Ghafūr* (the Oft-Returning)
- *al-'Azīz* (the Almighty)
- *al-'Alīm* (the All-Knowing)
- *al-Samī'* (the All-Hearing)
- *al-Khabīr* (the All-Aware)
- *al-Ḥamīd* (the Most-Praiseworthy)
- *al-Ghanī* (the Independent)
- *Shadīd al-'Iqāb* (the Severe in punishment)

In line with these descriptions the Qur'ān also brings home the following truths about Him:

- Allah knows all that is evident as well as hidden. Nothing escapes His notice. Given this, man should lead his life along the lines set by Him. Otherwise, man's misdeeds and unbelief will come to His knowledge and it will seal his fate in the Hereafter.
- He is man's only patron, protector and helper. Therefore, man should not turn to anyone else for help and support. Faith should draw him all the more to Allah, taking Him as the only source of all comfort and safety.
- The entire universe is created, governed and regulated by Him. Islam does not endorse the belief of some faith communities that after having created the universe, He no longer has any role in it. While

He does not normally interfere in the affairs of the world, which are subject to the laws of nature, He nevertheless watches all that happens and inflicts punishment on the guilty. In the creation and working of the universe, He did not draw upon anyone's assistance. All objects in the universe are subject to His command. His might and wisdom account for the perfect working of the interrelated yet complex and awe-inspiring natural phenomena. Had He not put such diverse things in place, chaos would have set in, bringing all life to an end.

- He alone is the Creator of all that exists. This underscores both His Oneness and creative power. Islam is very particular on its doctrine of monotheism. It differs sharply from the prevalent notions of a multiplicity or trinity of gods. Nor does it admit the role of some partner or assistant in creation. As the Creator, He knows well the needs of His creatures and provides sufficient sustenance for everyone. Furthermore, having created once, it is easy for Him to resurrect after death. This is what He would accomplish on the Day of Judgement. The amazing spectacles of birth, death and rebirth are there, all around us so that we grasp the basic truth and develop our conviction of faith.

- He exercises absolute authority over all that exists. It is He Who causes life and death. As part of His grand plan He executes what pleases Him. His authority is manifest everywhere. In recognition of His might man should worship Him. No one can alter His plan. Nor is it possible to defer or advance the time appointed by Him for anything. Since the domain of the Unseen is governed by Him alone, no one, including His messengers and angels, shares such knowledge. This further underscores His might and power.

- As He alone enjoys all authority, it is He Who passes judgement as He wills. No one can influence His judgement. Islam rejects false beliefs about intercession. For Allah alone decides everyone's fate, in line with His grand plan. On the Day of Reckoning He alone will reward or punish everyone. Notwithstanding His absolute power and authority, which cannot be challenged by anyone, His judgement is characterised by fairness and leniency. He does not take the guilty to task instantly. Rather, He keeps on granting respite. However, once the term of respite awarded to individuals and communities is over, no one can thwart His pronouncement. Moreover, His judgement is swift and marked by perfect justice. Reason demands that justice be done at the end of time in order to reward the pious and punish the guilty. For justice is not dispensed in this life. It is a common sight that the innocent suffer while the evil ones get away with their crimes in this world. It is therefore, both natural and logical that someone as mighty and powerful as Allah should sit in judgement finally so that everyone is recompensed.

- Allah's providing sustenance to every living being stands out as irrefutable proof of His lordship and power. Countless creatures, since the beginning of creation and up to the Last Day, have been, are and will be constantly fed by Him out of the inexhaustible resources created by Him. Moreover, there is His equally amazing distribution of provisions. One gets one's sustenance often from unexpected quarters. Allah makes no discrimination in providing sustenance, regardless of one's conduct and faith. Even His worst enemies are provided with all that they need in life. All this brings into sharper relief His forbearance, justice and wisdom.

- The entire universe represents a testimony to Allah's immense creative power. Natural phenomena, in particular, are evidence of His creativity and might. The Qur'ān cites some of these:

Surely your Lord is Allah Who created the heavens and the earth in six days, and is firmly established on the throne, regulating and governing all things. No intercessor can plead with Him, without His permission. This is Allah, your Lord. Therefore, serve Him. Will you not take heed?

(Yūnus 10:3)

Surely in the creation of night and day and in all that Allah has created in the heavens and the earth, there are signs for those who fear Him.

(Yūnus 10:6)

Allah sends down water from the heavens, and channels flow, each according to its measure.

(al-Ra'd 13:17)

And the earth! We have stretched it out and have cast on it firm mountains, and produced therein all kinds of things in due balance. And We have provided therein your means of living and also for those for whose sustenance you are not responsible. And there is nothing of which there are not with Us the treasures, and We send it down in a known measure. And We send the fertilising winds, then We send down water from the heaven, and We give it to you to drink ...

(al-Ḥijr 15:19-22)

Allah has sent down water from the heavens, then He revives the earth by it after its death. In this is a sign for those who listen. There is a lesson for you in cattle. From what is within their bodies, between excretion and blood, We produce for you a drink, milk, pure and pleasant to those who drink. And also there is a lesson for you in the fruits of date palms and grapes of which you take a wholesome drink and food. In that is a sign for a people who understand. And your Lord taught the bee to build its cells in hills, on trees and in men's habitations. Then you eat all manner of fruits and find with skill the spacious paths of the Lord. There springs forth from their bellies a drink, of varying colours, in it is a healing for mankind. In this is a sign for those who give thought.

(al-Naḥl 16:65-69)

On realising Allah's creative power, of which eloquent descriptions are scattered all around us, it is obligatory on man to affirm and celebrate His greatness and glory. As compared to Him, no one can lay any claim to majesty. For all living beings are mortal, subject to fall and decay. Even the unbelievers, who refuse to believe in Him, demonstrate their servitude to Him. For it is Allah Who causes their life and death and decides their fate. They are utterly helpless to resist His all-pervading authority. All objects of nature, bound to laws of nature, display their surrender to Him. For it is Allah Who makes them act in the way as it pleases Him.

Apart from being the sole Creator, Allah is man's guide and patron as well. He has blessed man with a body and physical faculties and invested him also with mental abilities, conscience and spirituality which help him in following the Straight Way. On the one hand, He has granted man free-will to choose the way he likes and on the other, He has made elaborate arrangements for man's guidance. He sent down a large number of messengers to every major community and geographical area for conveying the divine message to man. Furthermore, He revealed the Scriptures, embodying His extensive guidance for subsequent generations. The Qur'ān stands out as the latest and final divine guidance for all time and place. In this He spelled out clearly what pleases Him and what provokes His anger. Likewise, it also clarified, in many ways, what actions on man's part facilitate his admission to Paradise and what misdeeds land him in Hellfire. The way of life as approved by Him is demonstrated best by the Prophet Muḥammad's exemplary life. While acting on the message of the Qur'ān and following in the Prophet Muḥammad's footsteps one can win His pleasure and secure a place in Paradise in order to enjoy eternal bliss.

His mercy embraces all that exists. For without it, no one can survive. Were He to punish the guilty instantly, it would have brought an end to mankind a long time ago. Since He is Most Forbearing and Most Merciful, He overlooks man's sins and keeps on granting him extended respite so that he may mend his ways. His mercy alone accounts for all joy and happiness in this world. An amazing spectacle of His mercy will be witnessed by everyone on the Day of Judgement. Out of His kindness He will pardon many culprits and bless the pious ones, condoning their occasional lapses, with the interminable joys of Paradise. Only a very small part of His mercy is at work in the bond of love and affection between parents and children, spouses and family members and friends. Man should therefore, turn all the more to Allah, thanking Him for all His favours.

The Qur'ān states in several places that Allah accepts man's repentance, provided one turns to Him sincerely, invoking His mercy for pardon. He may even forgive man's worst sins, if he confesses his guilt, resolves never to repeat the same and lead a pious life onwards thereafter. More remarkably, it paves the way for one entering Paradise and enjoying bliss eternally. Many Qur'ānic passages point to His generosity in forgiving:

> *Do they not know that Allah accepts the repentance of His servants and takes their alms? Allah is undoubtedly the Oft-Returning, the Merciful.*
>
> (al-Tawbah 9:104)

One of the outstanding manifestations of His mercy and justice is that He rewards the pious. Obviously He does not stand in need of man's worship or obedience. However, so as to encourage good conduct, and ensure a happy, peaceful social life as also for man's spiritual development He has devised the principle of rewarding the pious and punishing the guilty. On the Day of Judgement He will recompense everyone in a manner characterised by perfect justice, fairness and generosity. His dispensation of justice is not flawed in any degree in view of His complete knowledge and His equal treatment of everyone. Piety alone weighs heavily in the scale of His dispensation. One's ethnic, family or linguistic affiliation does not concern Him in the least:

> *O mankind! We have created you from a single pair of a male and a female, and made you into nations and tribes, that you know one another (not that you may despise). Certainly the most honoured of you in the sight of Allah is he who is the most righteous of you.*
>
> (al-Ḥujurāt 49:13)

As for the relationship between man and Allah, the following features should characterise the same:

One should have overflowing love and respect for Him in view of His numerous favours and His magnificence: "*Those who believe are the strongest in love for Allah*", (al-Baqarah 2:165). Likewise, man should be thankful to Him for His countless bounties, for providing him with His guidance: "*O Believers! Eat of the good things that We have provided for you and be grateful to Allah*", (al-Baqarah 2:172). Constant thought of Allah should be present in man's mind, as part of his servitude to Him. Furthermore, it is the most effective means for keeping away from sin. It orients one's life to the goal of earning His pleasure which, in turn, guarantees success in the Hereafter. Allah's instructions on this count are clear:

> *Verily I am Allah! There is no god but I. So serve Me alone and establish regular Prayers to remember Me.*
>
> (Ṭā Hā 20:14)

Obedience to Allah should be the cornerstone of one's way of life. All that one thinks and does should be in line with His commands. This will render one as Allah's obedient, pious servant and ensure one's success in both worlds.

> *O men! Follow the revelation sent down to you from your Lord, and do not follow as friends or protectors any other than Him.*
>
> (al-A'rāf 7:3)

Since He alone is the only true Lord, without a partner or associate, help should be sought from Him alone. Allah has taught this to man in the opening *sūrah* of the Qur'ān, al-Fātiḥah: "*We serve only You and we seek help from You alone*", (al-Fātiḥah 1:5).

To sum up, one should devote oneself fully to Allah, in serving and worshipping Him, in abiding by His commands, and in leading one's life in accordance with the way prescribed by Him.

> *Truly my prayer and my service of sacrifice, my life and death are all for Allah, the Lord of the worlds. He does not have a partner. This I am commanded. And I am the first of Muslims.*
>
> (al-An'ām 6:162-163)

Related Qur'ānic passages for self-study

- Āl 'Imrān 3:26-27
- al-An'ām 6:95-104
- al-Anbiyā' 21:19-29
- al-Mu'minūn 23:78-92
- al-Nūr 24:35-45
- al-Furqān 25:45-50
- al-Naml 27:60-65
- al-Qaṣaṣ 28:68-70
- al-Rūm 30:20-27
- Ghāfir 40:61-68
- al-Shūrā 42:9-13

2

Allah's Messengers

Allah has certainly done a favour to the believers when He sent down among them a Messenger from among themselves, who recites to them His revelation, purifies them, and teaches them the Book and wisdom, while before that people had been in manifest error.

(Āl 'Imrān 3:164)

THIS concise Qur'ānic passage states who is Allah's Messenger, why he is sent down and what role and functions he performs. A clear understanding of this key Qur'ānic passage helps one grasp the Islamic concept of messengership and the important position of the Messenger in Islam, which is next only to that of Allah. Since the Messenger is central to faith, the Qur'ān spells out distinctly his status and the domain of his activities. This definitive Qur'ānic statement was also necessary in view of the prevailing misperceptions among the Arabs of the day about venerating their messengers beyond the permitted limit, even to the point of ascribing divinity to them. The most glaring such example is that of the Christians who mistook their Messenger Jesus, son of Mary as, God forbid, the Son of God. The Hindus too, have misconstrued messengers as the incarnation of God.

The Qur'ān dismisses such an outrageous proposition, asserting that it is beyond any messenger to lay claim to divinity:

It is not possible that a man to whom the Book has been given and wisdom and the Messenger's office, should say to people: "Be you my worshippers, rather than Allah's." On the contrary, he would say: "Be you worshippers of Him Who is truly the Cherisher of all."

(Āl 'Imrān 3:79)

"Allah does not ask you to take angels and prophets for lords and patrons. What! Would He ask you to unbelief after you have surrendered to Him?"

(Āl 'Imrān 3:80)

The Qur'ān makes a point of bringing out the humanness of all the messengers, especially the Prophet Jesus (peace and blessings be upon him). Take this statement as illustrative: "*Jesus Christ does not disdain to serve and worship Allah,*" (al-Nisā' 4:172). He is seen declaring: "*I am indeed a servant of Allah. He has blessed me with revelation and made me a Messenger,*" (Maryam 19:30). Significantly enough, almost all the messengers are introduced in the Qur'ān as Allah's servants, for example, Zakariyā (Maryam 19:2), Noah (al-Isrā' 17:3), David (Ṣād 38:17), Solomon (Ṣād 38:30), Job (Ṣād 38:41 and 44), Abraham, Isaac and Ishmael (Ṣād 38:45) and Muḥammad (peace and blessings be upon him) (al-Isrā' 17:1, al-Baqarah 2:23, al-Furqān 25:1, al-Kahf 18:1 and al-Ḥadīd 57:9). In all these instances, the messengers are described as *'Abd Allah* (servant of Allah). Likewise, the Arabs of the Prophet Muḥammad's day found it hard, rather impossible, to believe that a fellow human being could serve as God's Messenger. For them, it was too elevated an office to be held by a fellow human being.

The Qur'ān recounts the unbelievers' rejection of messengers on the grounds that they are ordinary human beings: "*There came to them Messengers with clear signs. But they said: 'Shall a mere human being direct us?'* So they rejected the Message and turned away," (al-Taghābun 64:6). The same point features in their remarks reported in the Qur'ān elsewhere (see Ibrāhīm 14:10, Yā Sīn 36:15, al-Shu'arā' 26:154 and 186, al-Isrā' 17:94, al-Anbiyā' 21:3, al-Mu'minūn 23:24, 33 and 47). The messengers, however, always presented themselves as human beings: "*Their Messengers said to them: 'True, we are human like you, but Allah grants His grace to such of His servants as He pleases*'," (Ibrāhīm 14:11). Of a similar import are the following Qur'ānic verses: al-Isrā' 17:93, al-Kahf 18:110 and Fuṣṣilat 41:6.

In sum, serious misgivings about the Messenger's humanness, his office and his role had been in circulation when the Qur'ān declared the above. This statement dispels all the mental cobwebs about this important institution, clarifying who the Messenger is and what he does by Allah's command.

The first and foremost point to be noted is that the Messenger represents Allah's invaluable favour to mankind. For, without the Messenger, mankind would have groped in error and ignorance. Man would not, of course, have found his own way to Allah, and as a result, he would have missed for ever such everlasting bounties from Allah as divine guidance, an excellent role model for leading one's life and deliverance in the Next. We must be thankful to Allah for having blessed us with His messengers in the same measure as we owe gratitude to Allah for providing us with the basic necessities of life, for example, air, water, food and parents.

That Allah's Messenger constitutes a divine favour for believers signifies that believers show their readiness to derive numerous and abiding benefits from the Messenger. On the contrary, the unbelievers follow the path of self-destruction in rejecting him. The believers greet his message and so doing they improve their prospects both in this life and the Next. Allah's Messenger, like any bounty of nature such as sunlight or rainfall is a source of immense benefit for everyone. However, only the believers make the most of his message. By opposing and rejecting him the unbelievers foolishly deny themselves a great bounty.

As to the Qur'ānic statement that the Messenger is "from among" the people whom he addresses, it stands out as yet another favour from Allah. Had the Messenger been from some other species, say an angel or *jinn*, it would have been impossible for people to follow in his footsteps. For, he would simply have been too different to be emulated in any degree. In his response system, his abilities and capacities, his performance level and his deportment, someone from another species would not have provided an inspiration for man to follow.

Likewise, if he had been from another community, ethnic, linguistic or cultural, it would again have posed problems. His "otherness" would have been a formidable barrier to accepting him. Nationalistic pride would have stopped people from paying any attention to him. Or the language barrier would have denied people's ability to mix with him. Furthermore, his alien socio-cultural profile would have kept people away from him. Allah provided a great favour to mankind in selecting the Messenger from among the people whom he first approached. Otherwise, people would not have drawn any benefit from him.

Take the example of the Prophet Muḥammad (peace and blessings be upon him) as illustrative. As a member of the leading family and tribe of Makkah and Arabia, and having lived for a full 40 years among his immediate addressees he was a thoroughly familiar figure locally. He knew first-hand the ailments afflicting his society. The Makkans enjoyed free, direct access to him and could communicate with him in their own language and at any time and place convenient for them. They could easily relate to him and in strict confidence. Likewise, they could verify his claims and conduct, without any difficulty. Unlike an outsider, he could not take them for a ride. That they could interact with him all the time was to their great advantage.

Under the Prophet Muḥammad's care and guidance, man learnt how to lead a purposive life, which, in turn, benefited the larger society. His sending down by Allah, no doubt, constituted a major favour. He instructed his followers in excellent morals and manners, spiritual development and flawless conduct. The role model afforded by him is a blessing for mankind for all time and place. For, following his example, man can attain the highest rank imaginable in both worlds. Viewed thus, his advent signifies Allah's immense favour.

What follows, in the Qur'ānic passage quoted at the outset of this chapter, is a pithy description of the Messenger's assignment, demonstrating his central position both in matters of faith and in man's individual and collective life. A messenger accomplishes, in the main, the following four life-enriching functions.

i. He preaches to man Allah's revelations.

ii. He purifies man.

iii. He teaches man the Book of Allah.

iv. He imparts wisdom to man.

i. Presenting Allah's message of guidance is his primary function, as is clear from his self-evident title of messenger. He conveys faithfully and vigorously the divine message to everyone. Transmitting the Word of Allah in its pristine purity is his main duty. This point is exemplified best by the Prophet Muḥammad's illustrious life. Even in the face of all the obstructions and persecution faced by him, he made a point of preaching the Oneness of Allah throughout his career. He dismissed outright any compromise on this vital issue. It is on record that he paid no heed to the pleas of his affectionate guardian and uncle, Abū Ṭālib, who, swayed by tribal affiliation, asked him to soften his stance on idolatry and polytheism. With his unflinching resolve the Prophet Muḥammad (peace and blessings be upon him) communicated each and every word of the divine message, which is codified as the Qur'ān. It enabled both his immediate addressees and later generations to benefit immeasurably from divine guidance. This divine arrangement of conveying eternal guidance through the agency of a messenger and preserving it until the end of time may thus be regarded as an outstanding favour extended by Allah. For it helps mankind identify and follow the Straight Way and win His pleasure and abiding success, particularly in the After-Life.

ii. The Messenger's other role consists in being a social reformer and spiritual mentor. Apart from preaching the Word of Allah, he sees to it that men imbibe its spirit in their individual and collective lives. Needless to add, this cannot be achieved without ensuring first their moral transformation and spiritual regeneration. These twin functions are performed by the Messenger. It is under his care that the believers manage to attain heights of moral and spiritual development. He instructs and guides them in every sphere of human activity, teaching them what is lawful and unlawful and instilling in them the belief that all their actions are closely watched by Allah. Since Allah is All-Hearing, All-Seeing and All-Knowing, they cannot escape Him in the slightest. Furthermore, since Allah embodies perfect justice, they are destined to be recompensed in all fairness and in full for their actions, both good and evil. Thanks to this pervading God-consciousness, believers make a point of thinking and acting only good. They thus turn into virtuous human beings, concerned solely with winning Allah's pleasure which alone brings about their deliverance. As a result of these teachings persuasively articulated by the messenger, believers are likely to achieve moral and spiritual perfection.

This is what really happened in seventh-century Arabia, as is graphically recorded in history. When the Prophet Muḥammad (peace and blessings be upon him) embarked on his mission, calling men to accept Allah's final and eternal message, the Makkan Arabs, his immediate addressees, enjoyed an unenviable reputation for their evil deeds, low morality and spiritual abasement. Under the Prophet's able guidance and affectionate care, however, these notorious people turned out to be such paragons of virtue, the likes of whom the world has not witnessed since or before them. These early Muslims or the Prophet's Companions stand out for their excellent character, their devotion to Allah, their commitment to truth, justice and equality, and their exemplary conduct. Their model behaviour, so to speak, cast a magic rather a magnetic spell on all those with whom they came into contact. It was one of the main reasons for the phenomenal spread of Islam even in far-off lands. Wherever these early Muslims went, they won over the hearts and minds of people, which resulted in the rapid expansion and consolidation of Islam. All this was possible only because of the model provided by the Messenger as an exemplary teacher. This underscores yet another of Allah's favours. Had Allah not assigned this role to the Messenger, the believers, in particular, and mankind in general, would not have known or scaled such heights of moral and spiritual elevation. Without the unblemished role model of the Messenger, mankind could not grasp or emulate the description of excellent conduct as spelled out in the Qur'ān, and which is expected of man by Allah.

The Messenger's function of purifying man resided in his instructing man to shun all that may pollute him physically, morally and spiritually. For he declared what is unclean for the body and asked the believers to avoid the same so as to ensure physical cleanliness and personal hygiene. More importantly, his teachings cleansed man of such abominations as idolatry, pride, this-worldliness and all other vices. He also instructed believers in attaining the sincerity and purity of intention. In sum, the Messenger discharged the function of a reformer of mankind.

iii. Another equally important function of the Messenger is his teaching and elucidating of the Word of Allah. His role is not of a mere courier who transmits the message. Rather, it is his assignment to elaborate the message in its finer details and to bring out clearly its import, dimensions and implications. This helps the believers grasp better its meaning. As men are of different intellectual calibre, it is important that the divine message be presented before them in an idiom best suited for them. Then, there are points in the Book in their abstract or theoretical form. It is the Messenger who demonstrates these to the complete satisfaction of people. Moreover, some points are open to more than one interpretation. Once again, the Messenger performs a key role in offering its correct interpretation, which saves people from falling into a trap or wandering in error.

The role of the Messenger as a teacher *par excellence* is illustrated by the Prophet Muḥammad's distinguished career. Throughout his twenty-three year long assignment as Allah's Messenger, his main preoccupation was the elaboration of the Qur'ān, the Book of Allah, for the benefit of those around him. His devotion to this task was so absorbing that on being asked to comment on the Prophet's conduct, his wife and close associate, 'Ā'ishah remarked that he exemplified in practice what the Qur'ān prescribes in theory. In doing so, the Prophet acted on the Qur'ānic directive issued to him: "*We have sent down unto you the Message; that you may explain clearly to men what is sent for them*", (al-Naḥl 16:44).

Had the Messenger only delivered the Book to the people, without any elucidation, or without setting his personal example, it would not have benefited people much. His advent as teacher may, therefore, be reckoned as Allah's favour to mankind.

iv. Besides expounding the Book of Allah, the Messenger imparts guidance and wisdom in a broad, general sense to believers, enabling them to mould their lives in accordance with the way prescribed by Allah. These instructions are rooted in the Book itself. As men face varied life situations and stand in need of divine guidance, the Messenger guides them at every step. This helps them follow steadily and consistently the Straight Way shown by Allah.

This life-enriching role of a mentor was accomplished by the Prophet Muḥammad (peace and blessings be upon him). He guided thousands of Muslims in his lifetime and more remarkably, his wise sayings (*aḥādīth*) and exemplary practice (*Sunnah*) have helped hundreds of millions of Muslims down the millennia. Needless to add, this guidance embraces the entire gamut of man's life. Thanks to the divine scheme of things, the wisdom imparted by the Messenger is characterised by such timelessness that it is as relevant and rewarding for mankind today as it was in the seventh century when he first presented these directives. His instructions have such a force and appeal as to transform the mindsets of believers even today.

To sum up, before Allah sent down His Messenger, who stands out as a perfect preacher, moral and spiritual reformer, teacher and mentor, mankind was steeped in error and ignorance: man must be thankful to Allah for this massive favour. For it is only with the help of the Messenger in transmitting, demonstrating and elucidating the divine message that man can follow the way approved by Allah.

Related Qur'ānic passages for self-study

- al-Baqarah 2:129, 151, and 212
- al-A'rāf 7:29
- al-Tawbah 9:33
- Ibrāhīm 14:1
- al-Naḥl 16:2
- al-Isrā' 17:92-95
- al-Kahf 18:55
- al-Mu'minūn 23:22
- al-Furqān 25:20
- al-Jumu'ah 62:2
- al-Ṭalāq 65:10-11

3

The Prophet Muḥammad
(peace and blessings be upon him)

Those who believe and do good deeds and believe in the revelation sent down to Muḥammad – for it is the truth from their Lord – He will remove from them their misdeeds and improve their condition.

(Muḥammad 47:2)

ALTHOUGH there exist many standard biographies of the Prophet Muḥammad (peace and blessings be upon him) in every major world language, the Qur'ān itself brings out the outstanding features of his illustrious life and career. Reading the Qur'ān one gets a clear picture of his message and mission and the central place he occupies in Islam. In the above quoted passage Muslims are promised forgiveness for their sins, if they follow the divine message sent down to the Prophet. This underscores the Prophet's coveted position in the sight of Allah. Without the pledge to abide by his teachings, no salvation is possible. His message is hailed as the truth revealed by Allah. More remarkably, Allah promises that one's commitment to it is bound to bring success in both worlds. For he is part of the chain of Allah's messengers who conveyed divine guidance to mankind. Rather, he stands out as the final Messenger, marking the end of messengership, (al-An'ām 6:85-90 and al-Aḥzāb 33:40). He belongs to the progeny of the Prophet Ishmael, son of the Prophet Abraham. His advent in seventh-century Makkah marks Allah's acceptance of the supplication made by the Prophets Abraham and Ishmael:

> *Our Lord! Raise up for them [the children of Ishmael] a Messenger from among them who will recite to them Your revelations and will teach them the Book and wisdom and will purify them [of sin and unbelief]. Surely You alone are Almighty, the Wise.*
>
> (al-Baqarah 2:129)

There is ample evidence to prove that he accomplished his four-fold mission well. At the time he appeared on the scene, the Arabs had discarded and corrupted the divine message conveyed to them by the Prophet Abraham. All sorts of evil – social, moral and economic – had crept into their way of life. They were given to drinking, causing bloodshed and sexual licentiousness. They had grown so callous that they used to bury their daughters alive. They had installed hundreds of idols in and around the Ka'bah and openly indulged in polytheism. As a pious person even in his pre-prophetic life, Muḥammad felt disturbed over the degeneration which he observed in his society.

When he was 40 years old, Allah appointed him His final Messenger, directing him to convey divine guidance in both word and deed. The Archangel Gabriel transmitted to him the opening verses of *Sūrah al-'Alaq*, which constitute the first installment of divine revelation. Throughout the 23 years of his Prophetic career he received at intervals its other parts, which taken together comprise the Qur'ān, the final Book of guidance for all mankind, regardless of time and place. His main assignment consisted in giving the good news to believers and warning unbelievers. At several places the Qur'ān projects him in this role. (See al-Baqarah 2:119, al-Nisā' 4:170, al-Mā'idah 5:19, al-An'ām 6:104, al-A'rāf 7:184 and 188, Hūd 11:2, al-Ḥijr 15:98, al-Naḥl 16:89, al-Isrā' 17:105, al-Ḥajj 22:67, al-Furqān 25:1 and 56, al-'Ankabūt 29:50 and al-Aḥzāb 33:45.)

He made plain his adherence to the Prophet Abraham's way with a view to reminding fellow Arabs of their original faith. So doing, he emphasised also the cardinal principles of monotheism in faith:

> *[Abraham declared] "As to me, I have set my face firmly and truly towards Him Who created the heavens and earth. Never shall I ascribe partners to Allah."*
>
> (al-An'ām 6:79)

The Prophet Muḥammad (peace and blessings be upon him) presented the essence of the creed of earlier messengers, asserting that he was there to confirm the Scriptures originally sent down to mankind. The Qur'ān stresses the essential similarity between its message and that of the Books revealed to other messengers. For all of these originated from the same source – Allah. Since earlier Scriptures had been corrupted by the wicked beyond recognition, there was a need to revive the original divine message. This task was performed by the Prophet Muḥammad (peace and blessings be upon him). Not only did he transmit faithfully the Word of Allah, he also demonstrated the way of life of a true believer. His distinguished life and conduct serve as the role model for all time and place. For example, Allah directed him to engage sincerely in worshipping Him in order to achieve closeness to Him. Moreover, he displayed exemplary bravery, courage and tact in overcoming the unbelievers on the battleground, (Āl 'Imrān 3:153 and al-Isrā' 17:74). These and many other points are cited in the Qur'ān in order to vindicate his genuine Messengership. The following passages, in particular, adduce arguments in support of his designation as Allah's Messenger:

- al-Baqarah 2:253
- Āl 'Imrān 3:68 and 162
- al-Nisā' 4:166
- al-Mā'idah 5:15-16
- al-A'rāf 7:181-182

- Yūnus 10:16-17
- Yūsuf 12:3 and 102-104
- al-Isrā' 17:86-88
- al-Naml 27:44-47 and 85-86
- al-'Ankabūt 29:48-52

Rather, Allah promised him the highest reward imaginable – that of elevating him to the station of praise and glory:

Your Lord will raise you to the rank of praise and glory.

(al-Isrā' 17:79)

And We have exalted your fame.

(al-Inshirāḥ 94:4)

Another of his distinctions is that he is the last Messenger in the chain of Allah's envoys. What this signifies is that Islam as revealed to and preached by him will serve as the final message for all time to come. The universality and timelessness of his mission are special to him, (Muḥammad 47:18 and al-Aḥzāb 33:40). As part of His grand plan for the guidance of mankind, Allah sent the Prophet Muḥammad (peace and blessings be upon him) down as the mercy for all the worlds, (al-Anbiyā' 21:107). Abiding by his directives amounts to obeying Allah. This underscores his pivotal position in matters of faith. *Ḥadīth* and *Sunnah*, his sayings and deeds respectively, are therefore, of the utmost importance in Islam and constitute the primary sources of faith. The Qur'ān commands Muslims to obey him unquestioningly:

And obey Allah and the Messenger, that you may obtain His mercy.

(Āl 'Imrān 3:132)

He who obeys the Messenger, obeys Allah.

(al-Nisā' 4:80)

He that obeys Allah and His Messenger attains the highest achievement.

(al-Aḥzāb 33:71)

Of similar import are the following passages, al-Mā'idah 5:92, al-Anfāl 8:2 and 64, al-Tawbah 9:71, al-Nūr 24:54, Muḥammad 47:33 and al-Taghābun 64:12.

Notwithstanding his many special features, the Prophet is a mortal human being, a servant of Allah, chosen by Him to convey His message to man. He does not share any trait of divinity. Nor does he have access to the realm of the Unseen which is only Allah's prerogative. The Islamic concept of messengership is marked by balance and moderation. Unlike Christianity, it does not elevate the Prophet to Godhead. And, unlike some other faiths, it does not project a tainted picture of messengers, given to worldliness and vice. In keeping with its cardinal principle of monotheism, the Qur'ān denies any suprahuman feature to him:

[O Muḥammad] Say: "I do not tell you that the treasures of Allah are with me. Nor do I know what is hidden. Nor do I tell you that I am an angel."

(al-An'ām 6:50)

They ask you concerning the Hour – when it is to come. Say: "Its knowledge is with my Lord alone. None can disclose its time but He" ... Say: "I have no power over any good or harm to myself except as Allah wills. Had I knowledge of the Unseen, I would have amassed all good and no evil should have ever touched me. I am only a warner and bring glad tidings to the people who believe."

(al-A'rāf 7:187-188)

The Prophet Muḥammad (peace and blessings be upon him) devoted himself heart and soul to the mission of Islam and achieved great success notwithstanding stiff opposition, in transforming the polytheistic Arabs into champions of monotheism. He drew upon every conceivable means for articulating the truth of Islam. His concern was so deep felt that he cried over the prospect of the inevitable divine punishment for those

Arab unbelievers who refused to embrace Islam. The Qur'ān, however, directed him not to grieve so much about the miserable fate of such unbelievers:

Perhaps you will kill yourself with grief because they do not become believers.

(al-Shu'arā' 26:3)

The Makkan unbelievers asked him to produce a miracle which they could see with their own eyes. They were told to look around them in that Allah's distinct signs are scattered everywhere. He was, nonetheless, granted the miracle which we know as the Qur'ān. For it embodies the light of Allah's guidance and mercy.

The Qur'ān recounts the prophecies about the Prophet Muḥammad's advent which featured in the earlier Scriptures, especially the Torah and the Gospels. Take this as illustrative:

And remember, Jesus, the son of Mary, said: "O Children of Israel! I am the Messenger of Allah sent to you, confirming the Torah, which came before me, and giving glad tidings of a Messenger to come after me. His name shall be Aḥmad."

(al-Ṣaff 61:6)

Even in the face of such clear pronouncements in their own holy Books about the Prophet Muḥammad (peace and blessings be upon him), the Jews and Christians of the day rejected and opposed him. They did so for their own selfish ends. For the radical message of Islam was set to destroy their vested interests, their degenerate way of life and their clergy that abused religion for pecuniary gain. However, Allah promised and sent His help to the Prophet. For example, when the unbelieving Makkans mocked him for being without a son, Allah consoled and comforted him:

To you We have granted al-Kawthar. Turn to your Lord in prayer and sacrifice. For he who hates you will be cut off [from future hope].

(al-Kawthar 108:1-4)

Allah blessed him with an overwhelming victory over the unbelievers, the Jews and Christians. Millions accepted Islam and country after country was won over to the Caliphs, who succeeded the Prophet, to lead the community of believers. As for the Prophet himself, he devoted more and more of his time to glorifying Allah and seeking Allah's forgiveness. As to the exalted rank which he enjoys in Allah's sight, the following Qur'ānic passage is instructive:

Allah and His angels send blessings on the Prophet. O Believers! Send your blessings upon him and salute him with all respect.

(al-Aḥzāb 33:56)

Allah also conferred another distinction on the Prophet – that of his Ascent and Night Journey to the heavens, which is recorded thus in the Qur'ān:

Glory be to Allah Who took His servant (Muḥammad) for the night journey from the sacred mosque to the farthest mosque, whose surroundings We have blessed in order that We might show him some of Our signs.

(al-Isrā' 17:1)

More importantly, on that occasion, he was granted the following charter of social justice, which also spells out the role and features of believers:

The believers are constant in their Prayer. And in their wealth there is a recognised right for the beggar and the poor... They respect their trusts and covenants. They stand firm in their testimony.

(al-Ma'ārij 70:23-25 and 32-33)

The same note of social justice permeates the Prophet's sermon at 'Arafāt which he delivered on the occasion of his farewell pilgrimage. It captures the essence of the mission which he professed and practised throughout his illustrious life:

No Arab is superior to a non-Arab and any non-Arab does not have superiority over an Arab. Piety alone confers honour on man. All men are from Adam and Adam was made of clay.

O people! Your lives, blood and property are sacred for one another ... All of you will certainly appear before Allah and He will take you to account. Thus do I warn you. Whoever among you is entrusted with someone's property shall return the trust to the rightful owner.

O people! Allah has laid down rights for everyone. No one should therefore, leave a will in favour of any of his heirs. Debt is to be repaid. Borrowed things are to be returned. It is not lawful to deprive anyone of what is due to him. Your wives have rights. They owe you obligations. Treat them well. For they are dependent upon you. If you follow the Book of Allah and my practice (*Sunnah*), which I leave behind with you, you will never go astray.

This sermon stands out as his strong exhortation for cordial human relationships and a tension-free society. His assertions about shunning violence and bloodshed, not usurping others' belongings and refraining from betraying the trust reposed in one re-echo the following Qur'ānic verses: al-Baqarah 2:283, Āl 'Imrān 3:161 and al-Nisā' 4:93. He is also seen reminding everyone of the need to discharge their obligations, especially those which they owe to fellow human beings in general and to their family members, friends and neighbours in particular. Man is asked to keep the trust placed with him as a responsible member of the society and as a good citizen.

Even in the face of his life-giving message and his spotless character and conduct, to which the Arabs had been a witness since his birth, many in and around Makkah took to opposing the Prophet. The pretexts they employed for rejecting his mission bordered on absurdity. For some of them took exception to his humanness, thinking that a fellow human being with whom they were familiar, could not be appointed to such an august office as that of messengership. They suffered from the delusion that only an angel or superhuman creature could shoulder this responsibility. In raising this objection they disregarded the point altogether that such a messenger could not relate to men and women for being radically different from them. Nor could he serve as a role model for them. Some were so overawed by his persuasive charms and magnetic personality that they dismissed him as a magician. No magician is, however, on record in history as striving for human welfare. Some alleged that he had borrowed material from others. They did not, however, identify his source or sources. Others regarded him as the author of the Qur'ān. Once again they remained blind to common knowledge that he was an unlettered person who could not draw upon earlier Scriptures. The ignorant Arabs could be forgiven in view of the general ignorance of articles of faith among them. However, even the Jews and Christians disregarded their own Scriptures which contain prophecies about his advent. Some sought to discredit him by branding him as a poet and the Qur'ān as the product of his mind. It was a silly charge. For no poet before or since has composed such a perfect book of guidance as is the Qur'ān. To those who demanded that some palpable miracle be given to the Prophet, which would convince them of the truth of his messengership, the Qur'ān told them that if they persisted in their unbelief, it would incur devastating punishment for them. The Qur'ān refutes the objections raised against his claim to messengership and asserts his exalted position. Muslims are directed to treat the Prophet with great respect and love:

> *O Believers! Do not put yourselves forward before Allah and His Messenger. But fear Allah. For Allah is All-Hearing, All-Knowing.*
>
> *O Believers! Do not raise your voice above the voice of the Prophet. Do not speak aloud to him in talk, as you may speak aloud to one another, lest your deeds go to waste while you do not perceive.*
>
> (al-Ḥujurāt 49:1-2)

> *You have indeed in the Messenger of Allah the perfect pattern of conduct.*
>
> (al-Aḥzāb 33:21)

Related Qur'ānic passages for self-study

- al-Tawbah 9:128
- Hūd 11:27
- Yūsuf 12:104
- al-Naḥl 16:46
- al-Kahf 18:27
- Ṭā Hā 20:2-3
- al-Qaṣaṣ 28:56
- Fāṭir 35:22-23
- al-Shūrā 42:13
- al-Ḍuḥā 93:1-11
- al-Inshirāḥ 94:1-8
- al-Kawthar 108:1-3

4

Life and Afterlife

Present before them the similitude of the life of this world. It is like the rain which Allah sends down from the heaven. The earth's vegetation absorbs it. But it soon becomes dry stubble which the winds scatter. And Allah prevails over everything.

Wealth and sons are the adornment of the life of this world. However, good deeds which last are best in the sight of your Lord as reward and excellent in respect of hope.

And beware of the Day when We shall remove the mountains and you will see the earth plain. And We shall gather them (mankind) all together. We shall not leave out anyone of them. And they shall be marshalled before your Lord in ranks. (It will be announced to them): Now you have come to Us as We created you the first time. You thought We should not fulfil the appointment made to you to meet Us.

And the book (of deeds) will be placed and you will see the culprits in terror because of what is recorded in it. They will say: "Ah! Woe to us! What a book is this! For it does not leave out anything, small or great. It records everything." They will find all that they had done. And your Lord does not treat anyone with injustice.

(al-Kahf 18:45-49)

WHAT is life? Is there any Afterlife? Are the two interlinked in any way? Questions such as these have agitated the human mind from the very beginning. As the divine message was forgotten and distorted by recalcitrant communities, many fanciful speculations gained currency about the nature of life in this world and the Afterlife. Philosophers, faith and community leaders and thinkers grappled, down the ages, with this issue in their own varied ways. In Hindu thought the purpose of life undergirds the cycle of birth and rebirth. By achieving the ultimate identity between the human self and the universal self, man may bring this cycle to an end. Buddhist thought rejects the concept of the universal self. Rather, the goal of life consists in suppressing desire and attaining a state of changeless tranquillity (*nirvana*). In modern Western philosophy life appears devoid of any meaning. The phenomenon of the Afterlife was denied by many including the ancient Egyptians, Hittites, Canaanites and Greeks. Some rule out the Afterlife outright, regarding the life of this world as an end in itself. At the other end of the scale, some dismiss this life and world as sheer illusion and prescribe asceticism and monasticism as the way out for attaining the joys of the Afterlife.

In the passage from the Qur'ān, quoted above, the issue is, however, resolved and the true nature of life in this world and its link with the Afterlife are explained. More importantly, it deals with the two in the context of man, clarifying that man's deeds in this life determine his status in the Next Life. Since it is a complex subject, the Qur'ān employs figurative language – parables, similes and metaphors for stating the Islamic stance on the issue.

What strikes one most in the above parable is that images are taken from ordinary, everyday human experience of the objects of nature – rain, vegetation, winds, and dry stalks left in a harvested field. This could easily be grasped by the immediate addressees of the Qur'ān – the seventh-century nomadic Arabs with a negligible literacy rate and also by people of later generations regardless of time and place. Another point worth mentioning about the Qur'ānic account is its note of balance and moderation. It neither condemns this world as an evil place nor rejects it as a mere illusion, recommending monasticism as a desirable way of life. Nor does it delink the present life from the Next, lending a sense of purpose and seriousness to the present life. The Qur'ān thus saves man from taking an extreme, fallacious position on this important issue.

The life of this world is one of Allah's major bounties. Life flourishes at Allah's command. As rain revives the dead land, filling it with thick foliage and pleasant vegetation, in the same measure Allah makes life full of charms and joys. Life must, therefore, be led only in the manner that its Master, Allah asks us to do. Notwithstanding its great attraction, the greenery around us should not blind us to its short life. Allah Who causes life to appear in its innumerable forms does and can reduce it to nothing in no time. The dense vegetation withering and decaying into dry, ugly stubble is a common sight. From this everyday occurrence man must learn the striking truth that all life is mortal, as brief as seasonal vegetative growth is. Equally significant is the truth that Allah being All-Powerful causes life to appear in its countless splendid manifestations and again, it is Allah Who ends it suddenly. Man should not therefore be carried away by the outward beauty of life. Rather, he should realise that life is temporary and that it is solely at Allah's command.

To illustrate the point further, the Qur'ān cites the concrete examples of wealth and sons who are extremely dear to man in this life. They are, no doubt, precious assets and a source of much joy. Yet they too, are as impermanent as seasonal vegetation is. Man cannot turn wholly indifferent to worldly objects. He is dependent upon them in leading his life. And precisely for the same reason has Allah blessed man with the basic necessities, especially wealth and children, sources of immense physical and emotional support and comfort. However, man should not be engrossed in these. Wealth and sons often distract man from strictly and consistently following Allah's way. Out of his love of wealth and children man is liable to do things which are not desirable in Allah's sight. The Qur'ān therefore, cautions man against this pitfall. Wealth and sons are not evil in themselves. For their outright rejection implies monasticism as the preferred way of life. Islam does not banish economic pursuits from the sphere of man's life. The Qur'ānic note of caution, nonetheless, is that man should not be given wholly to this world which might misdirect him away from Allah's path. In Islam these are rather the favours which Allah showers on man, and which render his life joyful and meaningful.

Man should, therefore, set his eyes firmly on the performance of good deeds which bring him Allah's pleasure. Wealth and sons may be deployed for achieving the same end. Significantly enough, Allah promises eternal reward and hope for deliverance for every good deed. Any particular deed is not specified on this count. It is evident from several *aḥādīth* that every good deed, permeated with the belief in the One True God, brings man nearer to Allah. This is what man's chief preoccupation in life should be. Although man and life itself are mortal, good deeds have a lasting effect, which may brighten man's prospects and exalt his rank in the Afterlife. Man should, therefore, realise this truth notwithstanding all the distractions and temptations in life.

As man is deluged by the numerous and enticing facets of life, which may make him negligent of the Afterlife and his eventual answerability to Allah on the Day of Judgement, the Qur'ān employs shock tactics by way of presenting a graphic, harrowing picture of the Last Day when the present order will be destroyed beyond recognition. Attention is first drawn to the devastating change in the landscape with which man is most familiar since his birth. Massive mountains, which man tends to regard as something permanent and fixed, will disappear altogether on the Last Day, reducing the earth to a plain, level field shorn of any structure such as trees and buildings. The truth is that nothing in the universe, including imposing mountains or the present landscape, is permanent. At Allah's single command the scenario will change completely.

Man is, no doubt, mortal. Yet his death is not some terminal point, signifying the end of everything. Rather, it marks his entry into the final phase of resurrection and retribution. All this might sound incredible to unbelievers and those given to materialism. Yet it is the truth that all men born and dead since day one until the Last Day will be brought back to life. The entirety of mankind, of all time and place, will stand in ranks before Allah. Among them will be the unbelievers as well, who contemptuously ruled out this eventuality. To their utter bewilderment and dismay, they would be told that notwithstanding their rejection of the Afterlife, they will have to face the final judgement and bear its terrible consequences. This is another truth of abiding value which man must imbibe throughout his life in this world – of his resurrection and of his accountability to Allah. Man should not disregard this even momentarily during his hectic life. For, on the Day of Judgement man will appear before Allah in the state He created him in the first place, dispossessed of all his worldly belongings, particularly his wealth and sons for whom he might have done something unlawful. His deeds alone will matter in the final reckoning. All worldly attainments, no matter how glamorous and coveted these might appear presently, will prove worthless. Man's good deeds prompted by his belief in Allah will carry weight.

In this context reference is made to man's record of deeds which is scrupulously maintained by Allah. This record will be adjudged on the Day of Judgement. This will add to the unbelieving sinners' anguish and distress. For it will contain full details of all their misdeeds. This is another truth which man should bear in mind for all his actions are being recorded and will serve as evidence against him in the final reckoning, the consequences of which will be long lasting. The perception of this important truth can help man shun sin and pursue the way shown by Allah. Worldly pursuits should not make him oblivious of this truth. The mass of first-hand evidence will decide man's fate on the Day of Judgement. For Allah, being the best of judges, will not treat anyone unfairly. The divine scheme of things is error-free and unbiased.

The most valuable element of this Qur'ānic passage is its elucidation of one of the major articles of faith in Islam – the Afterlife – in simple, easy-to-understand language and with the help of an appealing parable. Furthermore, the passage is remarkable for pressing home the following important points.

- Good deeds tinged with true faith alone ensure man's deliverance in the Afterlife.
- Sinners who do not have any good deed to their credit will realise their loss only when it is too late. It will aggravate their agony.
- Divine dispensation is transparently clear and fair. It is premised on the principle of equal opportunity. Each one of us has the opportunity and resources to perform good deeds in this life, which guarantee

rewards in the Next Life. Those who throw away this opportunity will regret it for ever.

- Life and the Afterlife are not some unfathomable mysteries. The former culminates in the latter. Life is thus a continuum; death is the line of demarcation between the two. Death does not represent the total end. Rather, man's deeds in this life will determine his reward or punishment in the Next Life. Life is temporary whereas the Afterlife is eternal. Life should not, however, be taken as some illusion. Notwithstanding its ephemeral nature, this life is part of the ultimate reality and has its lasting impact on man's fate in the Afterlife.
- The truth of the Afterlife and divine reckoning dawns on the unbeliever when it is too late. Man should therefore, grasp well the message of Islam contained in the Qur'ān and emulate the Prophet Muḥammad's role model. This alone can ensure his eternal happiness.
- Man should be ever-conscious of the Afterlife, especially his accountability to Allah on the Day of Judgement for each and every one of his deeds. This realisation being the essence of true faith should permeate man's mind and soul.

Related Qur'ānic passages for self-study

- Āl 'Imrān 3:10 and 14
- al-An'ām 6:94
- Yūnus 10:24 and 44
- al-Naḥl 16:94
- al-Isrā' 17:71-72
- Maryam 19:76 and 79-80
- Yā Sīn 36:12
- al-Zumar 39:21 and 69
- al-Shūrā 42:22
- al-Ṭūr 52:9-16
- al-Ḥadīd 57:20
- al-Naba' 78:17-20

5

The Qur'ān

And if you (O mankind) are in doubt about what We have sent down upon Our servant, then produce a sūrah *like it and call your witnesses or helpers besides Allah, if you are truthful.*

But if you cannot, and certainly you cannot [produce it], then fear the Fire whose fuel is men and stones. Hellfire is prepared for the unbelievers.

(al-Baqarah 2:23-24)

APART from stressing that the Qur'ān is a unique and inimitable Book, this passage defines the important concepts of the Scripture, Revelation and its bearer, Allah's Messenger. Such clarification was necessary as the Qur'ān was being revealed at a time when people held hazy notions about these. Most of the earlier religious communities did not possess any Scripture. For them, oral tradition served as their guidance. Some fallacious views however had crept into the beliefs of followers of even major world faiths who had been favoured with the Scriptures, especially as regards their source status. For example, the Jewish holy Book is reckoned as Scripture by Christians. Known popularly as the Old Testament, it forms part of the Bible. As opposed to this instance of the appropriation of one faith community's Scripture by another, there is yet another example at the other end of the scale. The Theravada Buddhist Scripture, the Tiptaka is taken only as a preparatory text by Mahayana Buddhists. For Hindus, the Bhagavad Gita is, no doubt, an important religious text yet it is not part of their Scripture, the Vedas. Besides Scripture, there have been serious misconceptions about the nature of divine revelation and its human recipient and the relationship between the two. On this count, the example of the Bible is most instructive. The Bible, though widely regarded as Scripture, took hundreds of years of compilation to receive this designation. No one can say with certainty which part of the Bible represents the exact Word of God and which is the product of its human scribes. More regrettably, for Christians, Christ has more meaning than the Bible.

In the above quoted passage, the Qur'ān presents a clear and cogent account of Scripture, divine revelation alone being its origin and content and the Prophet Muḥammad (peace and blessings be upon him) as its recipient being the one who faithfully transmitted it to mankind without having any role in its composition. The Qur'ān represents wholly the Word of God in its purity. In stating these articles of faith, the Qur'ān dispels all the prevalent misconceptions about Scripture which is the very basis of a faith community. More significantly, the Qur'ān declares that it is a miracle which is unique and inimitable. Also, it clarifies the relationship between the Word of God, the Qur'ān and its bearer the Prophet Muḥammad (peace and blessings be upon him) who is essentially God's servant. It leaves no room for confusion.

The passage is equally remarkable for the statements it declares, though initially directed at its immediate addressees, yet addressed to the whole of mankind. These are that

- The Qur'ān is the direct Word of God.
- It was sent down piecemeal to Allah's servant, the Prophet Muḥammad (peace and blessings be upon him).
- The Qur'ān is inimitable.
- No human being, individually or jointly, can produce anything like the Qur'ān.

- Those refusing to accept the above statement as true will be consigned to Hellfire.

Moreover, the passage vindicates the Oneness and Omnipotence of Allah, the Messengership as well as the humanness of the Prophet Muḥammad (peace and blessings be upon him) and the genuineness of the Qur'ān as the Word of God.

At the outset, it is declared that the Qur'ān is the direct Word of God. On this count the Qur'ān excels all existing Scriptures. For the latter have been distorted beyond recognition. It is impossible for one to distinguish between their divine and human components. By contrast, the Qur'ān has been preserved in its pristine purity since the day of its revelation up to the present time. It exists word by word exactly as it was sent down by Allah. Another striking feature of the Qur'ān is its gradual revelation, spread over around 23 years, which bears out its uniqueness. For it was sent down as the Book of guidance for an emerging community of believers in seventh-century Arabia. Circumstances changed dramatically during the course of its revelation. The community naturally needed clear instructions at each and every step. That the Qur'ān adequately catered for their ever-changing needs reinforces its divine credentials. For only the Word of God could steer a community in such trying circumstances. Furthermore, that the Qur'ān helped establish the invincible Muslim community and Islamic state and the splendid Islamic civilisation in Arabia during the brief span of only 23 years is another pointer to its miraculous nature. Only Allah's Book could accomplish all this in such a short time. Such a feat is without a parallel in history.

The Prophet Muḥammad (peace and blessings be upon him), servant of Allah is introduced as its recipient. This point is emphasised with a view to refuting misconceptions about his role in the authorship of the Qur'ān. Being a servant of Allah he regarded it as his greatest privilege to transmit it faithfully to his audience. As an unlettered person, not known for his literary or intellectual prowess in his pre-Prophetic life, he could not be credited with the composition of such a masterpiece as the Qur'ān is. However, blinded by their stubborn opposition to Islam, the unbelieving Arabs rejected the Qur'ān as the product of the Prophet's mind. In this passage they are asked to see reason and realise that the Prophet being Allah's obedient servant did not and could not ascribe anything to Allah which was not His. Notwithstanding this weighty argument adduced by the Qur'ān, even present-day detractors of Islam persist in hurling the same silly charge of dubbing the Qur'ān as the work of the Prophet Muḥammad (peace and blessings be upon him). It shows their ignorance of the phenomenon of divine revelation and their inability to note the marked distinctions between the human and the divine. In their malicious attempt to divest the Qur'ān of its divine origin, they betray their lack of discernment. A work as perfect as the Qur'ān could not be produced by the human mind.

Going a step further, the Qur'ān throws out an open challenge, asking the distrustful unbelievers to compose even one *sūrah* (chapter) like the Qur'ān. They are further told to seek the help of others, including those whom they imagine to be gods, besides Allah, in taking up this challenge. As part of this scintillating challenge the Qur'ān asserts that the unbelievers, both in the present and future, will never achieve any success in this attempt. History testifies that this Qur'ānic challenge has remained unanswered. Man should better realise that the Qur'ān is a miracle and that he is wholly subservient to Allah. Since this is the incontrovertible truth, man should not pursue further the path of falsehood or self-destruction which would land him only in Hellfire. Both the unbelievers and their idols made of stone will be the fuel of Hellfire. It will add to the unbelievers' anguish to see their idols beside them being roasted in Hellfire.

This dire warning rests on the premise that the Qur'ān is an unmatchable work. The unbelievers will never be successful in composing anything like the Qur'ān because it is characterised by numerous outstanding features. Of these, the following are worth mentioning:

- Unlike the palpable miracles granted to earlier messengers, which were specific to their time and place, the Qur'ān is timeless, relevant for all mankind until the end of time.
- The Qur'ān is inimitable in terms of its literary, linguistic and rhetorical excellence, a point conceded, in equal measure, by both

the seventh-century unbelieving Arabs and twentieth century Orientalists. Since its emergence on the scene, the Qur'ān has all along been the standard in the Arabic language and literature, against which all literary works are measured. In its vocabulary, usage, idiom, figurative language, literary devices, narrative techniques, textual finesse and stylistic features the Qur'ān is a work *par excellence*. Any human work pales into insignificance in comparison to its literary splendour and majesty.

- Notwithstanding its considerable length, consisting of more than six thousand verses, the Qur'ān stands out for its perfect coherence and cohesion. Unity of thought and singleness of purpose permeate and bind every part of the text. This distinction has never been achieved in any literary work composed by man. Some Qur'ānic scholars have conclusively identified this continuity of thought and thematic unity, featuring as it does like a thread, connecting one verse with the next and one *sūrah* with the next. Such thematic links appear more pronounced between the concluding part of one *sūrah* and the opening of the next. In sum, the Qur'ān is thematically an indivisible whole. Its distinct overarching worldview characterises its each and every part. Such amazing unity of thought and dexterity in introducing and developing intertwined themes is unimaginable in any product of the human mind. Moreover, the several layers of meaning as found in the Qur'ān are its other baffling characteristic. Readers of varying mental calibre grasp the meaning and message of the Qur'ān to their utmost satisfaction. Yet on each reading the Qur'ānic text yields new meanings. It would be pointless to look for such valuable elements in any human work.

- The Qur'ān is essentially the Book of guidance. In this respect, once again, it is unique. Contained in it are directives of abiding value both for individuals in their personal lives and for the society and community at large. Its scheme of instruction envisages every conceivable situation in which man might find himself – adversity or prosperity, war or peace, fear or hope, and a minority or majority condition. In all that the Qur'ān relates, especially of the history of earlier communities, the note of guidance for readers is always to the fore. It is to the Qur'ān's credit that its immediate addressees, the seventh century Arabs notorious for their evil ways and moral and spiritual degeneration, turned into role models of excellent conduct and enviable morals and manners. Their transformation, needless to add, was achieved, thanks only to the guidance imparted to them by the Qur'ān. More strikingly, the Qur'ān has continued to provide the same guidance to billions of people in every age, including our own times. No book can compete in any degree with the Qur'ān in terms of the perfect guidance it embodies for everyone – the rich and the poor, the old and the young, the specialist and the lay, the male and the female, and the ruler and the ruled. As an impeccable code of conduct governing every sphere of life, it instructs man comprehensively on how to live his life for the best, a way which will secure his deliverance and promote peace and happiness in the world. For its vast range of guidance benefiting every segment of society and for its indelible imprint on human lives the Qur'ān ranks as supreme.

That the Qur'ān is the infallible Word of God is borne out by the actualisation of its many prophecies. In the given circumstances these prophecies appeared as remotely impossible. The conditions of the day did not favour any of these. The unbelievers of the day took to mocking at these, taking them as wild flights of fancy. However, since these were announced by Almighty Allah, they came true in no time, much to the bewilderment of those who had rejected them outright. To illustrate the point, let us briefly examine just two such Qur'ānic prophecies:

i. In 615 CE *Sūrah al-Rūm* was revealed to the Prophet, with these opening verses:

> Alif. Lām. Mīm. *The Roman empire has been defeated, in a land close by; but they, after this defeat of theirs, will soon be victorious, within a few years. With Allah is the decision, in the past and in the future. On that day the believers shall rejoice, with the help of Allah: He helps whom He will, and He is Exalted in Might, Most*

> *Merciful. It is the promise of Allah. Never does Allah depart from His promise, but most men do not understand.*
>
> (al-Rūm 30:1-6)

As pointed out by 'Abdullāh Yūsuf 'Alī, this prophecy about the Roman victory was made

> when the tide of the Persian conquest over the Roman Empire was running strong. The Christian Empire of Rome had lost Jerusalem to the Persians, and Christianity had been humbled in the dust. At that time it seemed outside the bounds of human possibility ... that the tables would be turned and the position reversed within the space of eight or nine years.[1]

ii. While comforting and consoling the Prophet Muḥammad (peace and blessings be upon him) in the early Makkan period when the unbelievers ruthlessly persecuted him and even planned to assassinate him with a view to obliterating his nascent Islamic community, the Qur'ān promised him: "*We have exalted your fame,*" (al-Inshirāḥ 94:4). In the given circumstances, the Makkan unbelievers took this as a cruel joke. For he was then a lone figure, detested by his own tribesmen, including some of his own family members. By then only a handful of weak, resourceless people had responded positively to his call. Otherwise, he was widely dismissed as an outcast. Within a few years of the above prophecy, however, he reached the zenith of success, both spiritual and material. To this day he is universally acclaimed as the most successful religious figure, even by Orientalists given to Islam-bashing. The following glowing tributes paid by them point to the heights of fame scaled by him, as the Qur'ān promised:

"It does not seem too much to say that if any one man changed the course of history that man was Muhammad." (Charles Issawi, "Muhammad's Historical Role", *The Muslim World,* CT, USA 40 (April 1950, p. 95). "Of all men Muhammad has exercised the greatest influence upon the human race." (J.W. Draper, *History of the Intellectual Development of Europe*, London, 1864, 1, 329.) "Muhammad is the most successful of all Prophets and religious personalities." (*Encyclopaedia Britannica*, XVth edition, p. 898.) "Compare Muhammad with the long roll of men whom the world by common consent has called "Great". Take him all in all, what he was and what he did, and what those inspired by him have done, he seems to stand alone above and beyond them all." (Bosworth-Smith, *Mohammed and Mohammedanism*, London, 1874, pp. 339-340.) "Within a brief span of mortal life, Muhammad called forth, out of the unpromising material, a nation never united before, in a country that was hitherto but a geographical expression; established a religion which in vast areas superseded Christianity and Judaism and still claims the adherence of a goodly portion of the human race; and laid the basis of an empire that was soon to embrace within its far-flung boundaries the fairest provinces of the civilized world." (Phillip K. Hitti, *History of the Arabs*, London, 1948, pp. 121-122.)

These accounts give a fair idea of the veracity of the Qur'ānic prophecies. Needless to add, no human work can even be remotely compared with the Qur'ān on this count.

- The Qur'ān is basically a perfect moral code, urging man to profess and practise good and shun evil. It cautions man against all that is injurious to his moral, emotional, psychological and spiritual well-being. Its moral precepts infuse into man self-restraint, God-consciousness and purity in both word and deed. History bears testimony to the fact that the Qur'ān achieved remarkable success in changing the mindset of its readers. Unlike any human product, it is free from any flaw. Never before or since the revelation of the Qur'ān has any book attained the distinction of morally transforming billions of people.

- The Qur'ānic scheme of things, embracing life in this world and the Afterlife, is amazingly vast. It links the present life with the eternal life of the Hereafter. In so doing, it does not reject life in this world and man's concomitant obligations both towards God and towards his fellow human beings, whether his immediate family or humanity at large. Yet the Qur'ān asks man not to let his mind and heart swerve even momentarily from the thought of the Afterlife.

For the Qur'ān condemns materialism. Of all works, the Qur'ān alone holds the distinction of maintaining a fine balance between this life and the concerns of the Next. It is beyond the human mind to strike such a perfect amalgam. For many thinkers are on record as veering to the extreme of renouncing life altogether or taking this world as an end in itself.

- The Qur'ān prescribes the role model of exemplary behaviour in both theory and practice. Throughout his illustrious life, the Prophet Muḥammad (peace and blessings be upon him) exemplified what the Qur'ān preaches. On the one hand, the Qur'ān provides detailed guidance on every major moral issue, for example, verses 1-11 of al-Mu'minūn and 22-39 of al-Isrā'. On the other, it brings into sharp relief the living examples of historical personalities, both pious and evil. Contained in the Qur'ān, at one end of the scale, is the inspiring example of the Prophet Noah who preached his divine message for centuries and led a pious life. In a sharp contrast to him is his own recalcitrant son who defies Allah and incurs divine punishment. Some other outstanding examples of such vivid juxtaposition are the devout Prophet Abraham and his unbelieving father given to idolatry; the transgressing Pharaoh and his pious believing wife; the Prophet Adam and his wicked son; the Prophet Lot and his treacherous wife and the Prophet Joseph and his jealous brothers. These living examples facilitate man's instruction. Such forceful exemplification which produces a readiness in us to emulate is not to be found in any work authored by men of letters.

- The Prophet Muḥammad (peace and blessings be upon him) being an unlettered person who spent all his life in the narrow confines of Makkah, barring some trade journeys to Syria, could not and did not possess such an astounding knowledge of history, geography, law, and comparative religion which is embodied in the Qur'ān. The unmistakable divine origin of the Qur'ān is afforded by its internal evidence. Take for instance the contents of *Sūrah al-Kahf.* Sayyid Mawdūdī presses home the point thus:

After consulting with the People of the Book, the Makkan polytheists put three questions to the Prophet Muḥammad (peace and blessings be upon him) so as to test him. As for these questions, they were as follows: Who were the People of the Cave? What is the true nature of the story of Khiḍr? What is the story of Dhū al-Qarnayn? All these stories pertain to Judaeo-Christian history and were scarcely known to people in the Arabian Peninsula. The People of the Book had selected these stories carefully so as to test whether or not any extraordinary source of knowledge was available to the Prophet (peace and blessings be upon him). God subsequently provided adequate answers to their questions through the Prophet.[2]

- The Qur'ān surpasses all the books in the world for being the most widely-read book in existence. Translations of the Bible are, no doubt, available in most of the world's languages "yet the numbers who go through these in ten years is just a fraction of those who recite the Qur'ān every day".[3] Notwithstanding the intensely hostile and negative propaganda against the Qur'ān carried out by polemicists of all hues, Christian missionaries and Orientalists, the popularity of the Qur'ān has grown phenomenally with the passage of time. For billions of people it is the most sacred work on earth and their devotion to it is impressive. The respect and following commanded by the Qur'ān is unimaginable for any human enterprise. It is common knowledge that works paraded as ground-breaking, seminal and original grow outdated in no time. The Qur'ān has, however, retained its pivotal position among Muslims since the day of its revelation to the present day.

- The preservation of the Qur'ān for more than fourteen hundred years establishes, once again, its divine credentials, not shared in any measure by any other book. That the Qur'ānic text has remained intact even after fourteen centuries is acknowledged even by the Orientalists: "It is an immense merit in the Kuran that there is no doubt as to its genuineness. That very word we can now read with full confidence that it has remained unchanged through nearly thirteen hundred years." (Lane-Poole, *Selections from the Kuran*, Boston, 1879, p. 3.) "There is probably in the world no other work [except the Qur'ān] which has remained twelve centuries with so pure a text." (William Muir, *Life of Muhammad*, London, 1856, p. xxii.)[3] The practice of the Qur'ānic memorisation by Muslims throughout history has guaranteed the perfect preservation of the Qur'ānic text. No other book can boast of such an error-free arrangement for its preservation.

In sum, the Qur'ān is a miracle, the like of which cannot be imitated. The Qur'ānic challenge to produce anything similar to it has therefore remained unanswered to this day, vindicating as it does, its divine origin. The sooner man appreciates its numerous hallmarks and follows its life-enriching message, the better it will be. For only belief in the Qur'ān as the inimitable Book of Allah can save man against Hellfire.

Related Qur'ānic passages for self-study

- Yūnus 10:38
- Hūd 11:13
- al-Isrā' 17:88
- al-Qaṣaṣ 28:49
- al-Ṭūr 52:33-34
- al-Taḥrīm 66:6

References

1. 'Abdullāh Yūsuf 'Alī (Tr.), *The Meaning of the Holy Qur'ān*, Leicester, UK, Islamic Foundation, 2002, p. 401
2. Sayyid Abu'l A'lā Mawdūdī, *Towards Understanding the Qur'ān*, edited by Zafar Ishaq Ansari, Leicester, UK, Islamic Foundation, 1995, vol. V, p. 84.
3. Sayyid Abul Ḥasan 'Alī Nadwī, "Introduction" to *The Glorious Qur'ān*, translated by 'Abdul Mājid Daryābādī, Leicester, UK, Islamic Foundation, 2002, pp. xx-xxi.

6

al-Ghayb (the Unseen)

And with Allah are the keys of the Unseen. None knows it but He. And He knows whatever is on the earth and in the sea. Not a leaf falls but He knows it. Nor does a seed grow in the darkness of the earth without His knowledge. Anything fresh or dry is in a clear record. And He it is Who takes your souls by night and knows what you do by day. Then He raises you up again that the allotted term be fulfilled. In the end, to Him shall be your return. And then He will declare to you all that you did. And He is supreme over His creatures and He sets guardians over you until death overtakes one of you. Our angels take his soul and they never fail in their duty. Then all shall be taken back to Allah, their true Master. His shall be the decision and He is the swiftest in taking account.

(al-An'ām 6:59-62)

THE concept of *al-Ghayb* (the Unseen) has baffled many. In Islamic parlance it signifies "all that is unknown and is not accessible to man by the means of acquiring knowledge available to him. It refers to the realm that lies beyond the ken of sense perception".[1] The passage cited above mentions several items which belong to the domain of the Unseen – life, death and the Afterlife, the appointed term of one's life, angels, the Last Day, Resurrection and Judgement. These seemingly mysterious phenomena are elucidated in the light of Allah's attributes of knowledge and power. More importantly, the passage vindicates the truth of monotheism. Only the belief that there is One True God can help man fathom the mystery of the Unseen. Rather, in its light, the concept of the Unseen poses no difficulty for man. For the One True God stands out for His numerous perfect attributes. The passage draws attention to the following two – Allah's all-embracing knowledge and His absolute power to cause all that He wills. An understanding of these divine attributes enables man to grasp easily the phenomenon of the Unseen. Since Allah alone possesses all knowledge and power, man should not have any mental reservation in believing that He knows the Unseen and that He accomplishes all that pleases Him in view of His being All-Powerful. That perfect knowledge characterises Allah is repeatedly asserted in the Qur'ān:

> *Though it be but of the weight of a grain of mustard seed, and though it be in a rock, or in the heavens, or in the earth, Allah shall bring it forth. For Allah is the Subtle, the Aware.*
>
> (Luqmān 31:16)

> *He knows whatever was before them [His creatures] and whatever shall be after them. And they encompass nothing of His knowledge, except what He wills.*
>
> (al-Baqarah 2:255)

> *Allah it is Who has created the seven heavens and of the earth the like thereof. His command rules over them; so that you may know that Allah has power over everything, and that Allah encompasses everything in His knowledge.*
>
> (al-Ṭalāq 65:12)

As man assimilates and appreciates the truth contained in the above passages, he is most likely to develop a strong note of God-consciousness and piety which will help him steadily pursue the Straight Way prescribed by Allah. This will, in turn, ensure his deliverance. To sum up, for its stout vindication of monotheism, for its cogent elucidation of the divine attributes of perfect knowledge and power and for awakening man to the ultimate reality of man's death and accountability to Allah in the Hereafter, the passage quoted at the outset is of immense value and instruction.

It opens with a declaration that the keys or treasures of the Unseen rest with Allah alone. The choice of the expressions "key" or "treasure" in the context of something unknown as *al-Ghayb* heightens the meaning. More significantly, this assertion strikes a devastating blow against polytheism of every brand. No deity, spirit, angel or religious personality, including distinguished messengers and devout saints have any inkling of the Unseen. By dint of His perfect knowledge and absolute power Allah alone is the sovereign of this realm. This also repudiates the Trinity of the Christians, the dualism of Zoroastrian divinity and the pantheon of gods worshipped by pagans.

Throughout the passage there is a refrain-like reference to Allah's comprehensive knowledge, embracing the realms of both the Unseen and of the manifest as observable in this universe. The land and the sea are at His beck and call. So are the falling leaf and the seed in the depths of the earth. The falling leaf and the seed, represent, in a sense, the last and the first stage of existence. It is Allah Who knows and determines various stages of these and of everything in the universe and beyond. He knows perfectly well the seed and all that is inside the depths of the soil and also all that appears on earth and in the heavens. In sum, He knows the hidden and the manifest in perfect measure. Such extensive knowledge is not shared by anyone, including angels, messengers and saints. Allah is supreme and unequalled in terms of His knowledge. Others possess knowledge only to the extent Allah grants them. The Qur'ān makes this point emphatically and recurrently in order to refute polytheistic notions about the higher level of knowledge of messengers, saints and celestial spirits. Islam is absolutely clear on the point. Knowledge is special to Allah. He imparts it to His creatures in varying degrees, in accordance with their needs and as part of His grand plan.

Equally important is the need to realise the inexhaustible range of Allah's power, which is total and absolute. Like knowledge, power is granted in varying degrees by Him to His creatures as He deems fit. To give a fair idea of Allah's absolute power, the passage makes a pointed reference to some prominent facets of the Unseen – life, death and the Afterlife. With his limited sense perception man has been unable to fathom the mystery of life and death. It is Allah Who causes life and death at His will. That Allah exercises total control over man's existence is illustrated best by the everyday phenomenon of sleep and waking up. This is suggestive of life and death, caused by Allah. Regrettably, man pays no heed to this everyday re-enactment of the truth of life and death and rejects the doctrine of Resurrection. This alternation of falling asleep and waking up or of man's life and death goes on until a term preordained by Allah. Man has no knowledge of this. Nor does he have any means to ascertain the duration of this term. The exact term is known only to Allah, as its knowledge is related to the domain of the Unseen. Allah's attributes of perfect knowledge and absolute power are thus at work in man's everyday life. It is a great pity that man disregards this self-evident truth. That all living beings will eventually return to Allah is, once again, unmistakable proof of His knowledge and power. Needless to add, no one else can boast of such perfect knowledge and power, which can bring about the Resurrection of the whole of mankind and the Hereafter. More significantly, Resurrection is to be followed by Allah's reckoning. On account of His perfect knowledge and power He will bring back all the dead to life and declare to everyone all the deeds performed by him during his life in this world. It goes without saying that much of what one does is not known to others. It is hard, rather impossible to work out the exact deeds of earlier communities. This almost immeasurable chunk of information related to the Unseen, however, rests only with Allah. His creatures, including outstanding messengers, saints and religious personalities are only His "servants". He exercises total control and authority over them, as is borne out by their death and their resurrection at His single command. However, this truth will dawn on the unbelievers on the Day of Resurrection when they will see with their own eyes the spectacle of the grand assembly. With His unique knowledge and power Allah will summon this stupendous gathering.

The divine arrangement for appointing guardian angels for man and also for getting his deeds recorded faithfully reinforces Allah's absolute knowledge and power. With His massive resources Allah alone can devise such a bewildering scheme of posting angels for every human being. Like Allah's unquestioning authority over men, His control over angels too, is total and overwhelming. Angels are a special creature in their own right. Yet they are fully obedient to Allah and cannot and do not deviate even an inch from discharging the duties assigned to them by Allah. Of the numerous duties discharged by them, the passage makes specific reference to their guarding man, recording all of his deeds and seizing his soul as and when Allah commands them to do so. In spelling out all this the Qur'ān refutes the fallacious notions of the unbelieving Arabs and earlier communities regarding angels. Some mistook angels as gods; others as demi-gods. The seventh-century pagan Arabs of the Prophet Muḥammad's day audaciously looked upon angels as daughters of God. On studying the accounts of angelology and demonology one comes across several fanciful notions entertained about angels down the ages. Since the existence of angels belongs to the realm of the Unseen, about which man can only hazard conjecture, the Qur'ān makes a point of setting the record straight. In this and other passages, quoted below, the Qur'ān explains the nature, role and function of angels:

> *And before Allah bows whatever is in the heavens and whatever is in the earth of the living creatures and also the angels; and they are not arrogant. They fear their Lord above them and do what they are commanded.*
>
> (al-Naḥl 16:49-50)

> *O Believers! Guard yourselves and your family members against the Hellfire, of which the fuel are men and stones. Over it are angels, stern and strong. They do not disobey Allah in what He commands them, and they do what they are commanded.*
>
> (al-Taḥrīm 66:6)

> *Behold! When the two angels record, one on the right hand and the other, on the left. Not a word man utters but there is a watcher ready.*
>
> (Qāf 50:17-18)

Such clarification was all the more necessary in view of the prevailing Jewish and Christian misconceptions about angels. Take the following observation as illustrative of the distortions that had crept into the concept of angels even among faith communities, let alone that of pagans and unbelievers:

> The Old Testament nowhere lays stress on the moral character of angels. Consequently, angels were divided not into good and bad, but into those who worked wholly and those who worked only partly in obedience to God. The latter division still seems to hold its own in the New Testament alongside of the former.[2]

Allah's perfect knowledge and power come into play in the concluding observation in the passage that all living beings shall return to Allah for the Judgement. The divine recompense, of sending men to Hell and Paradise, is another important issue related to the realm of the Unseen. No one possesses this knowledge. Nor does anyone have the power to influence His judgement in any respect. The passage therefore, makes it patently clear that Allah alone will sit in judgement and that He will settle all cases in no time, which, once again, affirms His absolute power. Allah will judge everyone's record of deeds. This point is highlighted with a view to dispelling false notions about intercession which had gained currency by the time of the Qur'ān's revelation. People imagined that those whom they regarded as close to Allah would influence divine judgement. The most glaring instance on this count is that of the Christians, as is pointed out by 'Abdul Mājid Daryābādī:

> There is only Allah's decision, no other. This is specially to combat the Christian doctrine representing Christ as Judge. "The Son of man shall come in the glory of his Father with his angels; and then he shall reward every man according to his works." (Matthew 16:27) "When the Son of man shall come in his glory, and all the holy angels with him, then shall he sit upon the throne of his glory; and before him shall be gathered all nations; and he shall separate them one from another, as a shepherd divides his sheep from the goats; and he shall set the

sheep on his right hand but the goats on the left. Then shall the king say unto them on his right hand: Come, ye blessed of my Father." (Matthew 25:31-34) "That there will be a general Judgement is an article of faith. The Judge will be Christ." (*New Catholic Dictionary*, p. 523) "In the Gospels, while the Father is spoken of as the Judge, Christ's influence on the Judgement is also spoken of and more generally He Himself is Judge, and exercises this function on all men." (*Encyclopaedia of Religion and Ethics*, vol. 5, p. 325)[3]

By emphasising and pressing home Allah's perfect knowledge and power the Qur'ān removes all the doubts and misperceptions about the knotty issues of the Unseen and presents it as a concept which is easy to understand.

Related Qur'ānic passages for self-study

- al-Mā'idah 5:105
- al-An'ām 6:18, 38 and 108
- al-Tawbah 9:51
- Yūnus 10:30
- Yūsuf 12:40
- al-Zumar 39:7 and 42
- al-Jinn 72:26
- al-Infiṭār 82:10-12

References

1. Mawdūdī, *Towards Understanding the Qur'ān*, op. cit., vol. VII, p. 256.
2. *Encyclopaedia Biblica*, edited by Cheyne and Black. London, 1970, p. 168.
3. 'Abdul Mājid Daryābādī, *The Glorious Qur'ān*, Leicester, UK, Islamic Foundation, 2002, p. 261.

7

Creation

And recall when your Lord said to the angels: I will place a vicegerent on earth. They said: Will You place therein one who will make mischief and shed blood therein while we celebrate Your praises and glorify You? Allah said: I know what you do not know. And He taught Adam the names, all of them, then He set them before the angels, and said: Tell me the names of these, if you are right. They said: Glory to You! We have no knowledge except what You have taught us. Surely it is You alone Who are All-Knowing, All-Wise.

Allah said: O Adam! Tell them the names of those things. Then when he had told them the names of those things, Allah said: Did I not tell you that I know the secrets of the heaven and earth, and I know what you declare and what you conceal?
And recall when We said to the angels: Prostrate before Adam. They prostrated: not so Iblīs. *He refused and was haughty, and he became one of the unbelievers.*

(al-Baqarah 2:30-34)

THE question as to how this universe and its inhabitants, especially man came into being has always excited the human mind and imagination. For a faith community this issue is of the utmost importance. For the answer to this question and the beliefs about creation dictate the relationship of the universe with the divine and man's status and responsibilities. The stance on creation determines what life is, how man is expected to live it and what the ultimate end of everyone, including man is. In other words, such fundamental concepts as divinity, the purpose of life, man's role, the Afterlife and divine guidance hinge on a community's view of creation. It, thus, literally as well as metaphorically constitutes the starting point for the comprehension and appreciation of the universe, its nature and purpose, its Creator and its final end. The self-evident truth that the One True God is to be credited with the creation of the universe has, however, been clouded, rather eclipsed by fallacious notions held by various communities both in the past and in our own times, about the origin of life.

The Greek version concerns itself only with the birth of a plethora of gods and goddesses, making no mention of man's creation. Much more garbled is the account of *altjiranga* (the concept of creation in aboriginal religion), according to which heroic ancestors are regarded as the originator of life. In ancient Egypt, "Nun", (the primeval water) was credited with the phenomenon of creation. The first Book of the Old Testament, Genesis (Chapters 1-11) offers a detailed yet insipid version. The Biblical account runs as follows:

> In the day that the Lord God made the earth and the heavens, when no plant of the field was yet in the earth, and no herb of the field had yet sprung up – for the Lord God had not caused it to rain upon the earth, and there was no man to till the ground; but a mist went up from the earth and watered the whole face of the ground –
>
> (Genesis 2:4-6)[1]

On studying the above, the reader gathers the odd impression that man was created only for the purpose of "tilling the ground". Moreover, man does not seem to occupy any special place in the Biblical scheme of creation, for his birth is bracketed within the appearance of such ordinary objects of nature as plants and herbs. Nor was the earth provided with rain-water and plant life when man made his first appearance on the scene. In other words, scant attention was paid to meeting man's basic needs. The Biblical description of man's creation is devoid, in equal measure, of any outstanding feature:

> Then the Lord God formed man of dust from the ground, and breathed into his nostrils the breath of life; and man became a living being.
>
> (Genesis 2:7)[2]

By contrast, a couple of adjectives – "pleasant to the sight", and "good for food" – are employed for describing the tree of life.

In our times, under the pernicious influence of Darwinism, which maintains that the universe and all living beings have evolved over millions of years without any role for God, people have grown sceptical about the Scriptural version of creation. The Biblical account, in particular, is derided and pejoratively branded as creationism.

All such misconceptions are dispelled in the above Qur'ānic passage which offers a coherent, reasoned and appealing account of creation. Moreover, it brings into relief the following truths:

- Allah being All-Powerful is the only Creator. He brought everything into being out of His wisdom and no one has any share or role in it.
- Creation is not something haphazard or the result of the working of certain laws of nature. It stands out as a massive testament to Allah's creative power, and His grand plan, of which man is a key figure.
- Angels, a distinct species markedly different from human beings and *jinn*, are wholly obedient to Allah.
- Before Allah bestowed His vicegerency (*khilāfah*) on Adam, the progenitor of mankind, He blessed him with knowledge. This demonstrated Adam's excellence before everyone.

- Knowledge is special to man. Angels and other species cannot compete with man on this count. By utilising knowledge in the way prescribed by his Master and Lord, man can attain the highest degree of success.
- Satan deliberately disobeyed Allah out of pride. He stands eternally cursed for his deadly sins.

Being the Lord and Cherisher of mankind Allah has devised creation in such a perfect manner that it caters for all man's needs, especially physical and material. It has accordingly ensured man's survival on earth. It is nothing short of a miracle that the planet earth as created by Allah so long ago continues to provide adequately for man's sustenance. Needless to add, the human population has increased in astronomical proportions yet the same planet earth suffices for mankind. Its natural resources are so abundant that they appear to be inexhaustible. Apart from the provision of sustenance, and in line with His scheme of things, Allah has also arranged for the religious, moral and spiritual sustenance of man. Such guidance is imparted through His Messengers and Scriptures. Only Allah Who is the real Cherisher of mankind could draw up such a comprehensive plan for man's existence and guidance.

The Qur'ānic account of creation, as part of the Qur'ānic narrative strategy, is articulated in the above passage in the form of a dialogue between Allah and the angels. This dramatic mode is specially successful in immediately arresting the attention of its addressees. Moreover, the multiplicity of speakers brings about different perspectives which, in turn, enables the readers to form a much clearer, intelligent and reasoned view about the issue under discussion. The dialogue form, however, does not imply the co-equality of angels with Allah. Granted that the angels are seen in this passage making certain points. At the same time, they are found expressing unreservedly their unswerving obedience to Allah and pledging to glorify Him constantly, as is their wont. Their observation that the new species, man, after assuming Allah's vicegerency on earth, would indulge in violence and bloodshed, does not amount to calling into question divine wisdom. On the basis of the information they had gathered about the new species, man's constitution and temperament, especially his propensity to abuse the free-will granted him, they surmised it so. For, unlike them, man could choose to abandon the Straight Way and drift into error and wickedness. As faithful servants of Allah, the angels did not resent, in the least, the creation of this new species. Mawlāna Ashraf 'Alī Thānawī and 'Abdul Mājid Daryābādī offer the following rationale of the angels' mental reservations about man's creation:

> They said so not by way of protest or complaint but out of excess loyalty and devotion, as the most devoted bondsmen who could hardly bear their Beloved Master to employ a new servant besides them, for any of His services.[3]

The angels thus reiterated their unquestioning loyalty to Allah, emphasizing that they were prepared to carry out any assignment, however hard it might be. For their only concern was to celebrate Allah's praise and glorify His greatness. Both in their word and deed they were exclusively devoted to Allah.

In recounting the angels' response to the divine plan of creation, particularly to the appointment of man as Allah's vicegerent, the Qur'ān presses home the following important points:

i. The Qur'ān deflates the baseless notions of angelolatry (worship of angels as partners in divinity). At the same time, it refutes the equally pernicious idea of demonic or "fallen" angels, as features in the Bible. According to the Qur'ānic designation, the angels are:

> super-terrestrial, incorporeal, real and objective beings, not personified qualities and abstractions.... They are, in Islam, as unmistakably distinct from gods, as from men; and Islam knows no such things as fallen angels or degraded gods.[4]

ii. From man's constitution the angels had formed the opinion that he had a propensity towards violence. This, however, is only partly true. Under divine guidance and the messengers' training many men and women distinguished themselves, throughout history, as devout servants of Allah, without any major sin marring their record of deeds. They had no truck whatever with violence, bloodshed or any other evil. As opposed to Allah's perfect and all-embracing knowledge, angels possess limited knowledge. As a result, their inference was largely flawed. No one, including angels, has access to true and perfect knowledge. Man, in particular, is dependent on knowledge for leading his life. Out of His infinite mercy Allah gifted man with the requisite knowledge. The angels soon discovered that their apprehension about man's innate nature was not valid. Readily they sought Allah's pardon and forgiveness and realised that their knowledge was inadequate. In this lies an invaluable lesson for man. Like angels, man should be ever-conscious of his limited knowledge and his being no more than Allah's servant.

Of special importance in the above Qur'ānic passage is the concept of man's vicegerency. Needless to add, this concept is special to Islam. No other existing Scripture accords man such pride of place. Apart from "tilling the ground", the Bible assigns man the following:

> God created him; male and female He created them. And God blessed them, and God said to them, "Be fruitful and multiply, and fill the earth and subdue it; and have dominion over the fish of the sea and over the birds of the air and over every living thing that moves upon the earth."
>
> (Genesis 1:27-28)[5]

In sharp contrast to this, the Qur'ān bestows upon man the coveted status of God's vicegerent. This exalted rank obliges man to profess and practise sound beliefs, excellent morals and manners and live his life in consonance with the Straight Way shown by Allah. This vicegerency should not be misconstrued as the bestowal of political power and authority on every faithful servant of Allah. Nowhere does the Qur'ān promise Muslims political supremacy. Rather, their vicegerency consists in their striving to enforce Allah's will on earth to the best they can. In achieving this objective, political authority is, no doubt, helpful. Yet gaining political power is not an end in itself. Every believer should accomplish his assignment as His vicegerent by leading his life in total accordance with divine teachings and by trying his best to win Allah's pleasure. So doing, man, like angels, may celebrate Allah's praises and glorify Him. Of course, this also assumes engaging in liturgical worship directed at Allah.

In the above Qur'ānic account, Adam, the progenitor of mankind, stands out above the angels in terms of his superior knowledge, imparted to him by Allah. In recognition of the same the angels prostrated before Adam. As already indicated, the Qur'ān grants man the highest place in its scheme of things. Man's excellence lies in his ability to comprehend and appreciate in a discerning way Allah's infinite glory. While angels instinctively affirm Allah's greatness as part of their duty and temperament, man has the option to exercise his choice, of believing in or disregarding Allah. If he opts for the former, he establishes his superiority even over the angels. He is rewarded for making the choice which is the best one in the sight of Allah. However, if he chooses to reject Allah, takes others as partners with Him and fails to discharge his assignment of vicegerent on earth, he is doomed for eternal punishment and Hellfire. Viewed thus, creation is an integral component of Allah's grand plan of the universe. Since He is All-Knowing and All-Wise, He has chalked out such an all-embracing and logical scheme of things. Allah has charged man with these responsibilities in view of his potential and capacity to accomplish all this.

Another key concept introduced in this Qur'ānic passage is Satan, the embodiment of evil. Elsewhere the Qur'ān explicitly states that he is one of the *jinn* (al-Kahf 18:50), a species markedly distinct from angels (al-A'rāf 7:12). The above clarification deals a severe blow to the Biblical concept of Satan. For the Bible contains a detailed version of the former archangel, Satan's audacious revolt against God, his winning over one-third of all the angels in his battle against God and his sneaking into the Garden as part of his revenge, which culminated in the "fall" of Adam and Eve and their banishment from the Garden to earth. The Qur'ān puts an end to all these silly notions which make a travesty of Allah's power and knowledge and the role and status of angels. The Qur'ān, nonetheless, points to Satan's disobedience, which stemmed from his pride and megalomania. In Islamic tradition, therefore Satan is synonymous with evil. More importantly, man is alerted, throughout the

Qur'ān, against Satan, who is branded as his open enemy. Man should be constantly on guard against Satan.

This Qur'ānic passage on creation is remarkable for introducing the angels, Adam and Satan and for setting forth the seminal concept of man's vicegerency which, in turn, prescribes for man the right way of life, for reiterating the importance of knowledge and for providing an insightful description of Allah's creative power and perfect wisdom.

Related Qur'ānic passages for self-study

- al-A'rāf 7:11-25 and 206
- Yūnus 10:14
- al-Ḥijr 15:26-33
- al-Isrā' 17:61-65
- al-Kahf 18:50
- Ṭā Hā 20:116-128
- Fāṭir 35:39
- Ṣād 38:71-85

References

1. *The Bible: Revised Standard Version*, Swindon, UK, The British and Foreign Bible Society, 1971, p. 2.
2. Ibid.
3. Daryābādī, *The Glorious Qur'ān*, op. cit., p. 12.
4. Ibid., p. 11.
5. *The Bible*, op. cit., pp. 1-2.

8

Mankind

O mankind! Fear your Guardian Lord Who created you from a single soul, and He created from it its mate, and out of the two, spread many men and women. And fear Allah in Whose name you demand your mutual rights and the ties of kinship. For Allah ever watches over you.

(al-Nisā' 4:1)

THAT Allah brought the whole of creation into being is explained in the preceding chapter. We also there noted that man occupies the most significant position in the divine scheme of things and that he owes his birth, his life, his sustenance and everything to Allah.

The above passage now clarifies further the purpose of creation and man's relationship with his fellow human beings as Allah's creatures and as part of His grand plan. The creation of mankind manifests Allah's creative power. More remarkably, it underscores the unity of mankind in terms of common ancestry and the ties of kinship which bind men and women and other human beings together. The entirety of mankind represents a single interrelated entity with a common ancestor, identical purpose of life and dependence on Almighty Allah.

That Allah is the Only True God is the overarching message of the Qur'ān, permeating all its verses. It is not therefore, surprising that the Qur'ānic account of man's creation and later on, the emergence of a billions-strong mankind opens with the assertion about Allah being the sole Creator. Significantly enough, reference is made in this passage dealing with creation to Allah not simply as the Creator. Rather, He is presented as the Guardian Lord, a much more meaningful divine attribute. The point pressed home is that apart from being the Creator, Allah is also mankind's Guardian Lord, Who takes care of mankind's every aspect and need.

The pointed reference to Allah as the Guardian Lord in this context also aims at repudiating false notions of taking others as Allah's associates in creation. It is on record that several faith communities mistakenly credit their demi-gods, spirits, incarnations and heroic figures with the accomplishment of creation. In our own time, creation is usually explained away in terms of the theory of evolution. The Qur'ān brushes aside all these false ideas, asserting that it is Allah, the Guardian Lord Who has brought the whole of mankind into being. This truth is absolute, and hence no compromise can be made. Man should fear the All-Powerful Allah, if he refuses to believe in this self-evident truth.

Mankind's creation illustrates Allah's amazing and unrivalled creative power. The passage draws attention to the three modes of His creation. Each of these is equally bewildering and it should persuade everyone gifted with reason of His creative power and originality. The three forms of creation, as specified in the above passage, are: i) the creation of the first man – Adam from clay, ii) the creation of the first woman – Eve (Ḥawwā') from her mate, Adam and iii) the creation of mankind resulting from sexual union between man and wife. These three ways of birth are astounding, testifying as they do to Allah's inexhaustible creative power. It is easy for Him to cause man's birth in whatever way He likes. Of these three forms of creation, little is known about the first two, i.e. how Adam and Eve were born. For these two processes belong to the realm of the Unseen, to which Allah has not granted anyone access. By comparison, the normal reproductive process is common knowledge. While drawing upon Allah's gifts of reason and mental abilities man has managed to gather much knowledge about it. In the light of this knowledge man should feel all the more convinced about Allah's creative power.

In mentioning the birth of Adam, Eve and mankind the Qur'ān brings home another striking truth – mankind's unity or common ancestry throughout time and place. Contained in this Qur'ānic description are many significant points, of which the following deserve attention:

i. Notwithstanding the bewildering diversity in physical features, colours and languages as noticeable among mankind, all men, women, and children are the same and equal in being Allah's creatures. No one can lay claim to any special, privileged position on this count. All men are charged by Allah with the same set of obligations. They are entitled to the same reward or punishment for their performance. Allah does not discriminate against anyone in the slightest in all that happens to His creation. It demolishes baseless notions about ethnic or racial or class supremacy, as stated by Daryābādī:

> The Qur'ān repudiates the doctrine of polygenism, ascribing multiple ancestry to mankind, and incidentally also does away with the idea of castes or classes as forming a barrier to the common humanity. Contrast this with the Hindu concept that the Brahman is a caste derived from the gods, and Sudra (the outcasts/untouchables) from the demons.[1]

The following account throws further light on the class and caste system in Hinduism, which has wreaked havoc on the concepts of equality, dignity and social justice in society:

> The Rig Veda describes each of the classes coming from the body of the sacred primal person (*purusha*). The Brahamins came from his head, the thinkers of society; the warriors came from his arms, society's strength; the commoners came from his thighs, society's support, and the serfs came from the feet ... There are thousands of castes within India based on inherited profession and ideas of purity and pollution ... some castes are so polluting that they are called the "untouchables". Marriage between castes is strictly forbidden and transgressors are severely punished ...

Within a Hindu village castes are strictly segregated with the untouchables living beyond the village boundary.[2]

Given this, it is not surprising to note the Qur'ān condemning those guilty of fragmenting mankind into classes and subclasses, reducing vast chunks of humanity into hapless and helpless victims of oppression, injustice and poverty.[3] A glaring instance is afforded by the tyrannical Pharaoh, the ruler of Egypt who laid claim to divinity during the Prophet Moses's day:

> *Truly Pharaoh exalted himself in the land, and broke up its people into sections, weakening a party among them; their sons he slew but he spared their women. For he was indeed the maker of mischief.*
>
> (al-Qaṣaṣ 28:4)

ii. In the Qur'ānic worldview, variations in colour, ethnicity, language and other human features are mere tokens, facilitating identification. This diversity is part of the grand divine plan, which has lent colour and variety to life. These tokens should not be abused for establishing one's superiority over others. Rather, they should be better appreciated as signs of Allah's creative power:

> *Of His signs is that He created you of clay, and you are mankind, spreading yourselves. And of His signs is that He created for you from yourselves mates that you may find repose in them. And He set between you affection and mercy. In this are signs for a people who reflect. And of His signs are the creation of the heavens and the earth, and the variations of your languages and complexions. In this are signs for men of knowledge.*
>
> (al-Rūm 30:20-22)

According to the Qur'ān, all human beings are equal, regardless of their gender, colour, race or language. Fear of Allah or God-consciousness is the only criterion of one's superiority. For Allah has created man for the sole purpose of worshipping and serving Him. Therefore, he who performs this role best is the noblest of human beings, entitled to all honour in both worlds. The Arabs had been fed for centuries on false notions about their national and tribal pride and superiority. In line with the Qur'ān's message above, the following *ahādīth* strike a severe blow to such silly notions. While delivering his sermon on his Farewell Pilgrimage, the Prophet Muḥammad (peace and blessings be upon him) made this truth plain:

> O mankind! Listen! Your Lord is One and your ancestor is one. No Arab is superior to a non-Arab. No non-Arab is superior to an Arab. No white person is superior to a black person. Nor is a black person superior to a white one. One's superiority consists only in one's piety.[4]

He told Abū Dharr, his Companion: "You are no better than any white or black person unless you excel him in piety."[5] Equally instructive is his advice to his other Companion, Abū Hurayrah: "Allah does not look at your faces or wealth. He reckons your heart and your deeds."[6]

iii. Closely related to this radical Qur'ānic concept of the unity of mankind is the idea of gender equality, presented in the passage under discussion. For, the creation of Eve, the first woman, does not carry any stigma, as Daryābādī points out:

> This implies the essential equality of men and women as human beings. It was not in Islam, but in Christianity, to its eternal shame, that woman was considered 'an inferior, empty-headed moron; for several days in each month she was so unclean as to require secluding like a leper. The Council of Trent, in the sixteenth century, was dubious about her possessing a soul.'[7]

The Biblical account describes the creation of woman in terms which are both degrading and derogatory to her:

> Then the Lord God said, "It is not good that the man should be alone; I will make him a helper fit for him." ...
> To the woman God said: "I will greatly multiply your pain in childbearing; in pain you shall bring forth children, yet your desire shall be for your husband, and he will rule over you."
> (Genesis 2:18 and 3:16)[8]

In contrast, the specific reference in the Qur'ānic passage to the womb, symbolic of motherhood, underscores women's elevated and honourable status in Islam. This proclamation was all the more radical in pre-Islamic seventh-century Arabian society. For these pagan Arabs regarded women, including their mothers and wives, as no more than any other saleable commodity. Mothers and wives were and could be disinherited by male heirs, reducing them to an utterly destitute state. They had no share in their father's or husband's inheritance.

In addition to the above general directive that man should be aware of the Ever Watchful Allah in his dealings with women, the Qur'ān has enacted an elaborate law of inheritance, establishing once and for all that womanhood is no bar to inheritance. Indeed the Qur'ān fixed her specific share as mother, wife, daughter and sister.

Mankind has increased manifold as a result of the sexual union between men and women. In view of their common ancestry and their mutual attraction and love, the Qur'ān exhorts them to base their family and broader social life on the noble principle of observing and maintaining ties of kinship. Several *aḥādīth* urge that one should faithfully discharge the obligations one owes to one's parents, brothers and sisters, wives and children and other relatives. Its range also extends to treating one's neighbours and fellow human beings in general well. Allah has sanctified these ties, as is evident from the passage under study. For it speaks of Allah as the Ever Watchful Lord. Any neglect of these obligations on man's part will incur Allah's displeasure. Accordingly, the passage is prefaced with the exhortation to fear Allah. A true believer who is always conscious of Allah cannot disregard these social ties. It is in man's own interest to reinforce such ties of kinship. Needless to add, it facilitates warm, cordial social relations and peace and joy in life. The exhortation to honour ties of kinship recurs throughout the Qur'ān. Take the following passage as an instance in point, in which those violating this bond are condemned:

And those who break the covenant of Allah after its ratification and cut off what Allah has commanded to be joined and act with corruption in the land, upon them is a curse. For them there shall be the evil abode.

(al-Ra'd 13:25)

In view of its insightful coverage of man's social life, especially interpersonal relationships among human beings, the Prophet Muḥammad (peace and blessings be upon him) used to recite this passage while solemnising marriage. For it reminds man of his social obligations towards both his near and dear ones and towards the broader community of human beings around him. It is perhaps needless to say that one who sincerely takes Allah as his Guardian Lord is most likely to discharge his social and familial obligations as specified in this passage. Its moral precepts are an excellent guide for man in his social relations and for appreciating his bond with all human beings.

Related Qur'ānic passages for self study

- al-Baqarah 2:27
- al-A'raf 7:189
- al-Naḥl 16:72
- al-Rūm 30:21
- al-Aḥzāb 33:6
- al-Zumar 39:6

References

1. Daryābādī, *The Glorious Qur'ān*, op. cit., p. 156.
2. *Chambers Dictionary of Beliefs and Religions*, edited by Rosemary Goring, Edinburgh, UK, Chambers, 1992, p. 89.
3. Daryābādī, *The Glorious Qur'ān*, op. cit., p. 156.
4. *Musnad* of Imām Aḥmad, vol. 5, p. 411.
5. Ibid., p. 150.
6. Muslim, *Ṣaḥīḥ*, "Kitab al-Birr".
7. Daryābādī, *The Glorious Qur'ān*, op. cit., p. 156
8. *The Bible*, op. cit., pp. 2-3.

9

Prayer (*Ṣalāh*)

Remember Me; I will remember you. Be grateful to Me and do not deny Me. O Believers! Seek help with patience and Prayer. For Allah is with the patient ones.

(al-Baqarah 2:152-153)

PRAYER (*Ṣalāh*) being one of the five pillars of Islam is mentioned many times in the Qur'ān as an obligatory duty for every adult Muslim. It is to be offered five times a day and certain prerequisites are to be met before offering it. In the above Qur'ānic passage, however, the focus is on the essence or underlying spirit of prayer, which helps one grasp this basic duty and pivotal concept in Islam.

Needless to add, prayer in some form features in every religious tradition. Some of its popular forms are: incantations, spells and devotional acts and rituals. It varies from being silent to vocal, often assuming the form of meditation. In Christianity, it

> is Prayer to God the Trinity; to the Father, through the Son, by the Holy Spirit. It may include elements of adoration, confession, intercession, petition or thanksgiving, following the pattern of the so-called "Lord's Prayer" which Jesus taught his disciples

> (Matthew 6:9-15, Luke 11:2-4) and other biblical examples of prayer, especially those found in the New Testament epistles and the Old Testament psalms. Use is also made of the prayers of saints and spiritual writers. Posture in prayer varies. Some traditions teach kneeling, some standing, some sitting ... Forms and types of prayer also vary.[1]

By comparison, monotheism permeates both the concept and form of prayer in Islam, as it is devoted wholly to Allah, the One True God. Like any other Muslim, the Prophet Muḥammad (peace and blessings be upon him) performed the same prayer, bowing and prostrating to Allah. Furthermore, unlike other faiths which recommend private or public forms of prayer, which usually turn into exercises in inner contemplation or meditation, Islam prescribes prayer as an obligatory duty, to be performed in congregation in a mosque, a particular structure set apart for this specific purpose. It is to be offered at appointed hours and in a particular manner, of which details are to be found in the Qur'ān and *Ḥadīth*, and as exemplified by the Prophet Muḥammad (peace and blessings be upon him). His Companions faithfully followed the way he said Prayers and the same has been the practice of billions of Muslims down the ages. Remarkably, its form and features have remained unaltered all along. Every Muslim performs it alike at the same hours, regardless of the place of his residence and in the same direction of Makkah. Both literally and symbolically prayer has been the most distinct bond of Muslim fraternity in all time and place.

Certain prerequisites must be fulfilled before offering prayer. For example, the washing of some body parts is a precondition for prayer, (al-Mā'idah 5:6). If one is in a state of impurity, one should take a bath, (al-Nisā' 4:43). Likewise, one should put on clean clothes when offering Prayer, (al-A'rāf 7:31). One should also face the direction of prayer, (al-Baqarah 2:150). It is imperative that prayer be said at its appointed hours – at dawn (*Fajr*), at noon (*Ẓuhr*), in the afternoon (*'Aṣr*), after sunset (*Maghrib*) and in the late evening (*'Ishā'*), (al-Nisā' 4:103, Hūd 11:114, al-Isrā' 17:78-80 and Ṭā Hā 20:130-132). It is preferable and more rewarding to pray in congregation, (al-Baqarah 2:43 and al-Nisā' 4:102).

Some other conditions governing prayer are that Allah's excellent names and attributes be mentioned and a portion of the Qur'ān be recited in prayer. Furthermore, the Qur'ān recitation should be in a distinct tone, (al-Isrā' 17:110, al-'Ankabūt 29:45 and al-Muzzammil 73:4). An extensive account of these and other norms to be observed during prayer feature in standard works on Muslim theology and jurisprudence. The passage we are concerned with here examines only the spirit of prayer defining what it is, its components and its benefits for man. For its better appreciation this passage should be read together with the following Qur'ānic extracts which bring into further relief the objectives and essence of prayer:

> *Successful are the Believers, those who humble themselves in Prayer.*
>
> (al-Mu'minūn 23:1-2)

> *And seek [Allah's] help in patience and Prayer. Surely it is hard, except for those who fear Allah.*
>
> (al-Baqarah 2:45)

> *Those who pray, they are constant in their Prayer, and in whose wealth there is a portion for the beggar and the poor. They testify to the Day of Judgement and are fearful of their Lord's punishment.*
>
> (al-Ma'ārij 70:23-27)

> *Woe be to such performers of Prayer, who are negligent of their Prayer, who aim to be seen and who withhold even common items from others.*
>
> (al-Mā'ūn 107:4-7)

The passage selected for study and cited at the outset opens with the exhortation that man should remember Allah. Since He is man's Creator, Sustainer and Benefactor *par excellence*, it is perfectly in order that man's mind and heart be filled with the thought of His majesty, glory and numerous favours.

More importantly, such deep consciousness of Allah and His excellent attributes should be reflected in man's total, unquestioning obedience to

Him. One should make a point of discharging, to one's level best, the obligations with which Allah has charged one. In other words, one should exert oneself in trying to live life in accordance with the way shown by Him. One may recite certain liturgical formula, as recommended in the *Ḥadīth* corpus, as part of one's remembrance of Allah. Yet what is more important is that one's entire life and all of one's deeds should conform to the example approved by Him. Such remembrance, unlike the five obligatory Prayers, is not time-place specific. Every act done with the intention to win Allah's pleasure belongs to the same rubric of remembering Allah. It is equally applicable to a careful study of the signs of Allah scattered in and around the universe. For such a study carried out objectively, and without any misperception, convinces man all the more of His inexhaustible creative power, glory and benevolence. Of the various modes of remembering Allah, the above one is the most fruitful and befitting. During the golden era of Islamic sciences, culture and civilisation Muslims were fired by the same ideal of identifying and glorifying Allah's creative power. As a result, they made a substantial contribution during the early part of Islamic history to all the then branches of learning, particularly medicine, geography, mathematics and natural history.

In sum, remembrance of Allah does not consist only in chanting some liturgical formula in a devotional ambience. It signifies an outlook on life and a mindset which makes one constantly think of Allah, especially His greatness. As a result, man is engaged in such acts which please Him.

That Allah remembers those who are devoted to Him represents His promise and incentive in order to reward them. In the present life a devout person may or may not be blessed with His abundant provision. However, it is certain that he enjoys peace of mind, contentment of heart, tranquillity of soul and a sense of purpose, rather, mission in life. In the Next Life, he is destined for all the joys of Paradise, ranging from palatial houses to the best quality of food and drink and things which are presently beyond man's imagination. Allah's remembrance of man is the highest felicity imaginable for man. Since Islam is the natural way and universal faith, even this highest honour is open to anyone. It is not earmarked for any particular family, race, time and place, colour, gender or class. Anyone, by dint of his piety, may acquire such an exalted position. As an incentive, held out by Almighty Allah, this should be grabbed with the utmost urgency. It is undoubtedly a high return premium, which must not be neglected.

Besides remembering Allah, man must express his unstinted gratitude to Allah, for He has provided man with numerous bounties – material, spiritual and intellectual. It perhaps goes without saying that man cannot even count the favours granted to him by Allah, let alone thank Him for each of these. Yet being grateful to Allah

> is a basic religious value in Islam. Man owes thanks to God for almost an infinite number of things. He owes thanks to God for all that he possesses – his life as well as all that makes his life pleasant, enjoyable and wholesome. And above all, man owes thanks to God for making available the guidance, which can enable him to find his way to salvation and felicity.[2]

Fulfilling the demands of faith, particularly those arising out of the belief in monotheism, may thus be equated with expressing thanks to Allah. The most befitting way to do so is to spend all that man has received from Allah – his life, his mind, body and heart, his financial resources, in sum, his entire life – in Allah's way. It is on record how the Prophet Muḥammad (peace and blessings be upon him) and his Companions set noble examples of the same. Reports state that Abū Bakr, the Prophet's closest associate offered all his possessions for the fund raised by the Prophet (peace and blessings be upon him) in Islam's cause.

The directive for remembering and thanking Allah is enforced by cautioning man against unbelief which consists in being unthankful to Allah. This underscores the importance of thanksgiving. For any laxity in doing so might draw one closer to unbelief. Likewise, neglecting to remember Allah impels one to indulge in evil, in ascribing partners to Him, and even to denying Him altogether. The Qur'ān condemns unbelievers mainly for abusing the faculties granted to them by Allah for rejecting Him. It is, no doubt, the height of ungratefulness to turn against one's Master and Benefactor and to use the resources provided by Him for opposing Him.

Remembering Allah, expressing profuse thanks by word and deed to Him and avoiding anything which might even remotely amount to unbelief underscore the concept of prayer in Islam. It is in this sense that the passage under discussion encapsulates the spirit of prayer. Another distinctive feature of prayer is invoking Allah's help and support for everything and in every aspect of life. One should seek, in particular, His mercy and forgiveness for success in this life and deliverance in the Hereafter. Prayer thus is the most effective and energising means for maintaining and strengthening one's link with Allah. Since man is liable to disregard this important truth of his total dependence on Allah in the hurly-burly of life, prayer is a prescribed duty to be discharged as many as five times a day. That one should fulfill the preconditions before offering prayer, aims once again, at enhancing man's consciousness of Allah. The more one turns to Him, the better it is for one's own interest.

The description of prayer as invocation is meant to comfort and console man. In life one is liable to face many hardships, sorrows and calamities. For man does not have any control over the course of events, no matter how carefully he might plan things. Despite one's best efforts one does not necessarily achieve the goal dearest to one. Seen against this backdrop, prayer stands out as the most desirable source of relief and assurance and as a ray of hope and confidence in the all-round darkness. For, while praying one recounts one's plight to Allah, Whom one believes in as the All-Powerful and All-Merciful. One prays with the realisation that He will show one a way out, either immediately in this life or reward one in the Hereafter for all one's sufferings.

It is an immensely comforting exercise, relieving one of much anxiety and pain. Offering prayer, particularly in a crisis, boosts one's morale, providing one with the strength and courage to take on problems.

Professing and practising self-restraint by way of putting up with suffering and overcoming temptations is yet another great blessing which one derives from prayer. For it infuses such patience and self-discipline that one does not digress from Allah's way. Even in the face of temptation one behaves in a restrained way, keeping one's emotions and feelings under control. In Qur'ānic parlance, patience is a very broad, all-encompassing virtue of the mind and the heart. It is not to be taken in the narrow sense of bearing with a pain, physical or emotional. One is free to express one's sorrow and suffering. Islam does not forbid this. What Islam does, however, disallow is loss of trust in Allah as one faces some crisis. Prayer instructs man in reposing faith in Allah. This fills man with the courage and confidence to take on all hardships. More remarkably, (i) it instils into man such deep God-consciousness and keen self-discipline which helps him control his base desires, (ii) prompts him to obey Allah in every walk of life and (iii) enables him to bear with adversity in the hope that Allah will reward him for his perseverance. The Qur'ān portrays such a persevering person in the following glowing terms:

> *It is a virtue to believe in Allah and the Last Day, and the angels, and the Book and the Messengers; ... to be firm and patient, in pain and adversity and in time of violence.*
>
> (al-Baqarah 2:177)

Patience is to be displayed, especially during times of sickness, poverty and war. It is a virtue rated highly throughout the Qur'ān. A person practising self-restraint is promised entry into Paradise and Allah's mercy and company, (al-Baqarah 2:155 and 249; Āl 'Imrān 3:146, al-Anfāl 8:46 and 66 and al-Zumar 39:10). The close link between patience and prayer is illustrated best by the Prophet Muḥammad's role model. Whenever he was confronted with adversity, he would rise to pray which filled his heart with tranquillity.

After bringing out these features which comprise the spirit of prayer – remembrance of Allah, thanksgiving to Him, shunning polytheism, invoking His help and practising self-restraint – prayer is finally mentioned as being synonymous with

- a deep consciousness of Allah
- imbibing humility
- acting with self-restraint and self-discipline
- avoiding any disobedience of Allah

- fulfilling one's obligations to both Allah and one's fellow human beings
- generosity towards the poor and the needy
- gaining firm faith
- fear of Allah
- turning to Allah in a crisis, and
- looking forward to His rewards

To be more precise, prayer is identical with the virtue of patience (*ṣabr*), for the prayer posture itself signifies obedience to Allah. Prayer also keeps one away from all evil and enables one to invoke His help and support.

As in the opening verses of *Sūrah al-Mu'minūn* and verses 23-35 of al-Ma'ārij, in the passage under study too, the Qur'ān makes a point of spelling out the rewards accruing from prayer. The person offering prayer along the recommended lines is promised the highest reward, that of enjoying Allah's company. It is indeed a covetous reward. The main point driven home is that prayer imbues man with the moral courage and strength to withstand the turmoils of life, to reject all temptations and digressions and to perform consistently such acts which win Allah's pleasure. It is not therefore, surprising that prayer occupies pride of place in the scheme of life drawn by Islam. For prayer is the only duty in Islam which one is obliged to perform not once, but as many as five times a day. By comparison, other obligatory devotional acts have to be offered much less frequently. Its regular offering is aimed at instilling the many virtues emanating from it, into the character and conduct of believers. Moreover, throughout the Qur'ān, there is emphasis on discharging this duty, and on its appointed hours and in the requisite form and spirit.

Of Prayer's numerous benefits, the one mentioned in the passage under discussion is that of being blessed with Allah's company. It goes without saying that being Omnipresent Allah accompanies everyone all the time. Special to the believer, however, is the moral strength, courage and spiritual power which he gains as a result of maintaining his close ties with his Lord. That it boosts morale is illustrated by the example set by the Prophet's Companions. These early Muslims, though lacking in resources, managed to outdo their much better equipped opponents. Take the Battle of Badr as an instructive case in point. In this battle, the Muslims, though vastly outnumbered, managed to overwhelm their enemy, the unbelieving Quraysh and record a stunning victory which defied the logistic superiority possessed by their enemy's army. Implicit in enjoying Allah's company is the idea that true believers receive His help and support which keeps them steady on the path of faith and purity.

Those offering prayer, characterised by the above features, are branded as the persevering ones. One so endowed is promised the invaluable reward of enjoying Allah's company. This divine promise with its unmistakable spiritual dimension, represents an enviable reward. May Allah enable us to reap these and many more rewards from offering prayer devoutly and regularly.

Related Qur'ānic passages for self-study

- al-Baqarah 2:45
- al-A'rāf 7:128
- al-Mu'minūn 23:1-10
- al-Ma'ārij 70:23-35

References

1. *Chambers Dictionary of Beliefs and Religions*, op. cit., p. 441.
2. Mawdūdī, *Towards Understanding the Qur'ān*, op. cit., vol. II, p. 306.

10

Fasting

O Believers! Fasting is prescribed for you, as it was prescribed for those before you, that you may become God-fearing. Fasting is for a fixed number of days. But if any of you is ill or on a journey, the prescribed number of days should be made up later. For those who can fast with hardship, their redemption is the feeding of a poor person. But who does good, of his own free-will, it is better for him. And it is better for you that you fast.

Ramaḍān is the month in which the Qur'ān was sent down, as a guide to mankind and with evidence; one of the Books of guidance and judgement (between right and wrong). So everyone of you who witnesses the month should fast, and whoso is ill or on a journey, for him is the like number of other days. Allah intends every facility for you. He does not want to put you to difficulties. So you should complete the number and glorify Him for His having guided you. And perchance you may give thanks.

Permitted to you on the night of the fast is the approach to your wives. They are your garments and you are their garments. Allah knows what you used to do secretly among yourselves; but He turned to you in mercy and forgave you. So now approach them and seek what Allah has ordained for you, and eat and drink, until the white thread of dawn appears to you distinct from its black thread. Then complete your fast till the night appears. And do not approach your wives while you are in devotional retreat in mosques. These are the bounds of Allah. Do not go near these. Thus Allah makes clear His signs to mankind that they may fear Him.

(al-Baqarah 2:183-185 and 187)

THIS single Qur'ānic passage offers a comprehensive account of the major aspects of the second pillar of Islam – fasting. Some of the points addressed are: why fasting is prescribed; how long one must fast for, what its exemptions, allowances and redemption are, what occasioned the practice of fasting; how to make up for missed fasts; what one is allowed and forbidden in a state of fasting; what its underlying spirit is and what some of its benefits are.

Although the address is direct and categorical, comprising a set of specific commands, it takes into account human concerns and limitations. Apart from being a series of commands which are interrelated, the above passage addresses both the human heart and mind. Its unmistakable thrust is that fasting is an effective means for imbibing, developing and reinforcing God-consciousness. It is not therefore surprising that fasting is prescribed as a duty for every adult Muslim. Reading the above passage one readily grasps the form and essence of fasting in Islam.

The passage introduces fasting as a widely recognised concept with which every faith community is familiar. Since divine revelation originated only from Allah, the One True God, it is not surprising that fasting has all along been an integral part of worship:

> The practice of abstaining from food or drink for religious purposes may be for a long or for a short time. Different religions prescribe different fixed times for fasting ... Fasting is often prescribed as preparation for special ceremonies, duties or activities, or as penance.[1]

Monotheism, however, is the outstanding feature of the Islamic concept of fasting. It is for Allah alone, in recognition of the numerous bounties bestowed by Him. Of these, special mention is made of the Qur'ān, the perfect divine Book of guidance, in the context of thanksgiving. Further, it is affirmed that fasting helps man turn wholly to Allah. As in prayer, the focus in fasting too, is on Allah. *Aḥādīth* state that Allah has promised His choicest rewards for those who fast faithfully. Take this observation made by the Prophet Muḥammad (peace and blessings be upon him) as an instance in point: "The smell of the mouth of a fasting person is more agreeable to Allah than the smell of musk." The orientation of fasting for Allah is special to Islam. For, in other religious traditions, both the concept and practice of fasting have been corrupted:

> Both the Jews and the Christians took to fasting as a mere mode of expiation or penitence, or for purposes even narrower and strictly formal. 'In olden times fasting was instituted as a sign of mourning, or when danger threatened, or when the seer was preparing himself for a divine revelation'.[2]

On studying Jewish tradition, it emerges that

> there are six fast-days in Jewish tradition. Four of these commemorate phases of the Babylonian devastation ... The fifth fast-day occurs on 10 Tevet marking the beginning of the Babylonians' siege of Jerusalem in 587 BC.[3]

More intriguingly, the sixth fast, known as the Fast of Esther, was prescribed by Esther, an ordinary Jewish woman selected by the Persian king, Ahasuerus, to be his queen on account of her beauty. While planning her revenge against Haman and securing a favour from the king she proclaimed:

> Go, gather all the Jews to be found in Susa, and hold a fast on my behalf, and neither eat nor drink for three days, night or day. I and my maids will also fast as you do. Then I will go to the king, though it is against the law; and if I perish, I perish.[4]

As opposed to such narrow ethnic concerns, fasting in Islam appears as an intensive spiritual exercise, touching upon every aspect of man's life in this world and devoted wholly to Allah the Creator and Sustainer as thanksgiving. As pointed out by Daryābādī, fasting in Islam:

> is a voluntary and cheerful renunciation, for a definite period, of all the appetites of flesh lawful in themselves, a salutary exercise of both the body and the spirit. 'Disciplinary fasting', such as Islamic fasting may be termed, 'is regarded as a reasonable and useful practice, even by those who consider all other forms of fasting to be misconceived and vain. Normally, it is a reasonable part of the soul's preparation for the maintenance of self-control in times of strong temptation'.[5]

In another Western reference work on comparative religion, the Islamic concept of fasting draws the following accolade:

> This is a tremendous discipline, especially in places where the temperature becomes very hot during the day, and it gives unity to Muslims throughout the world because they know they are all sharing the Fast together. It represents a sacrifice, a limitation upon indulgence, and a kind of purification; it is also a moral symbol of the need to empathize with the sufferings of the hungry throughout the world.[6]

Amid the many features of fasting, self-restraint lies at the core of this exercise. It is common knowledge that in His infinite wisdom Allah has forbidden only a few items of food and drink, for example, pork and wine. Barring these, man is free to partake of the numerous items provided by Him as these are perfectly lawful and wholesome. A believer, no doubt, acts with self-restraint in observing the Islamic dietary law. However, fasting calls for greater self-restraint. For a fasting person is not allowed to take in even a small quantity of all that is lawful. For a month during the daytime he is obliged to refrain from eating, and drinking anything or having sexual relations with his wife. All that is forbidden, however, becomes once again lawful for him after he breaks his fast. The entire exercise hinges on the laudable values of self-discipline, self-restraint and self surrender. Not only in his dietary habits, but also in his everyday life, especially social and moral, the same principle of self-restraint becomes more strictly applicable in governing his conduct during fasting. Islam urges Muslims to refrain from every misdeed that disturbs the social fabric:

> *O Believers! Let not one group mock another group. It is likely that the latter may be better than the former. And let not some women mock other women. It is likely that the latter may be better than the former. And do not defame one another nor be sarcastic to one another. Do not call one another by (offensive) nicknames. Ill is the name of sin after one has affirmed belief. And those who do not desist, they are wrongdoers. O Believers! Avoid suspicion as much as possible. For suspicion in some cases is a sin. And do not spy on one another, nor speak ill of one another behind their backs. Would any of you like to eat the flesh of his dead brother? You would abhor it.*
>
> (al-Ḥujurāt 49:11-12)

While fasting, it is a greater abomination to commit any of the above misdeeds. The Prophet eloquently warned Muslims that their fasts, vitiated by their indulging in any evil act, would be rejected outright by Allah as null and void. He clarified that Allah does not desire that His servant should stop eating and drinking for a few hours. Rather, His pleasure consists in observing him living a pious life. Fasting is an effective exercise to achieve this end.

That the spirit of self-discipline permeates fasting and that it, in turn, strengthens a closer and stronger tie between man and Allah is a recurring point in the Qur'ānic passage about fasting under examination. It describes the following as the fruit of fasting: "... that you may become God-fearing", that "you should glorify Him for His having guided you", that "... you may give thanks", and "that they (men) may fear Him".

Islam envisages an act of worship essentially as man's direct, intimate contact with Allah. This feature is prominent in prayer, fasting, pilgrimage, *Zakāh* and all forms of supplications, chants and invocations to Allah. Man is supposed to turn only to Allah and to implore Him from the depths of his heart, with the belief that he is in one-to-one contact with his Lord. At the same time, nonetheless, all these acts of worship in Islam have a distinct collective and social dimension. They have a public face and appear as a community activity, with its bearings on all fellow Muslims. These acts go a long way in inculcating and cementing cordial social relations and in promoting such virtues and values as fraternity, mutual help and bonds of unity and familial ties. This unique blending of the personal and the social or the individual and the collective is to the fore in both the concept and practice of fasting.

First, it infuses a keen sense of unity and bonding, as Muslims the world over fast during the same period. The additional prayers after *'Ishā'*, known as *Tarāwīḥ*, offered in large congregations, broaden and intensify the bond.

Charity is much encouraged in Islam. During Ramaḍān, the month of fasting, its reward increases manifold. The Prophet is on record as having stated that a good deed performed while fasting brings one 70 times more reward. Prompted by such exhortations, Muslims generously give in charity during Ramaḍān. Most of them make a point of disbursing *zakāh* money in the same month. It is worth noting that feeding the needy is prescribed in the Qur'ānic passage under study as the expiation for those who are unable to fast. It is also not out of place to mention in this context *Ṣadaqah al-Fiṭr* (Charity to be given before offering *'Īd* Prayer which marks the conclusion of Ramaḍān). All this, perhaps needless to say, contributes to generous spending in Allah's cause, i.e. helping the poor and needy. Fasting thus reinforces the practice of charity in society.

In stating that fasting was an obligatory duty for earlier believing communities, the Qur'ān affirms the identical divine origin of all faiths. All the messengers presented the same call to truth to their respective communities, which was revealed to them by Allah. However, men tampered with divine teachings and fragmented themselves into various sects. The Qur'ān, while confirming in principle the existence of earlier Scriptures, offers the latest and unaltered version of divine teachings.

Let it be clarified that the Qur'ān points only to the identical concept of fasting in earlier faiths. As to its finer details, Allah has enacted such commands in varying times which fit in best with the local conditions of each faith community. The detailed regulations of fasting in Islam are not therefore, necessarily the same as those which were valid for earlier communities.

The Qur'ān spells out elaborate regulations as to how Muslims should fast. The first notable point is that fasting is for 29 or 30 days in a calendar year, corresponding with Ramaḍān, the ninth month of the lunar calendar. Islam being the natural way makes due allowance for man's limitations and constraints. Accordingly, it grants exemption to certain people who are unable to fast. They belong to two main categories: (a) the terminally ill, the old and the infirm who cannot fast and (b) those on a journey or who fall ill. As a consequence, they cannot fast for a few days during Ramaḍān. The former are exempted from fasting. They are directed to seek redemption by feeding the needy. The latter are advised to make up the prescribed number of fasts by observing them at a later date, after Ramaḍān.

What occasioned the practice of fasting in Islam is firmly stated in the Qur'ān. Since Islam is a universal faith, relevant for all time and place, fasting is not linked with any event of local/Arab or Islamic history. Nor is it related in any way to the Prophet Muḥammad (peace and blessings be upon him) in his personal capacity. It was during the month of Ramaḍān that the Qur'ān, Allah's biggest favour to mankind, began to be revealed. Fasting thus represents thanksgiving on man's part for being blessed with such perfect guidance as is contained in the Qur'ān. We must also clarify immediately that the Qur'ān was sent down piecemeal, spanning a period of over 22 years. The first passage, the opening verses of *Sūrah al-'Alaq*, was sent down during Ramaḍān and hence its commemoration by way of fasting. The link between Ramaḍān and the Qur'ān is emphasised in the Prophet's directives to the Muslim community. In line with the same, Muslims make a point of reciting the whole of the Qur'ān, both individually as self-study or collectively by joining congregational *Tarāwīḥ* Prayers on Ramaḍān nights. The Qur'ān introduces itself as the Book of eternal guidance for the whole of mankind.

It draws attention to its two outstanding features – its universal import and its role as the source of Allah's guidance. These features are reflected in its categorical commands which help man derive guidance and discern between good and evil, and right and wrong.

While laying down the regulations for fasting, especially those governing the old and the sick, the Qur'ān invokes the following directive principle: "Allah intends every facility for you. He does not want you to be put to difficulties." This point comes out sharply in the remaining part of the verse. In following the guidance shown by Allah and His Messenger man can glorify and praise Allah.

Likewise, by reflecting on the numerous signs of Allah's creative power and wisdom, man can turn into Allah's grateful, obedient servant. That He has prescribed fasting, which is of immense benefits for man, and that He has made allowances for those who cannot fast should evoke man's thanks and praise to Allah.

The next regulation, of abstaining from sex while fasting and of resuming it at night, emphasises once again the note of self-restraint and total surrender to Allah as being the outstanding features of Islam. For, sex which is perfectly lawful is disallowed during fasting. Another striking feature of the passage is its elucidation of the Islamic concept of gender relations and sexual conduct. The permission to Muslims to enjoy sexual relations on Ramaḍān nights indicates that in Islam sexual activity can co-exist well with the sacredness of Ramaḍān. Islam affirms a close, intimate relationship between man and wife, represented through the metaphor of the garment in the Qur'ān. According to Daryābādī:

> The metaphor is of exquisite beauty, expressive of close intimacy, identity of interest, mutual comfort and confidence, the mutual upholding of each other's reputation and credit, the mutual respect of one another's secrets, mutual affection, and mutual consolation in misfortune ... The wedded pair ceases to belong to themselves; they now belong to each other, sharing each other's joys, sorrows, glories and shame.[7]

The Qur'ānic description of gender relation in terms of man and wife being each other's garment does not establish in any way one's superiority over the other. Nor does it betray any note of misogyny, relegating woman to an inferior position. Daryābādī cites the Qur'ānic position as so in order to drive home the following significance:

> Compare this with the attitude of Christianity which holds the woman as an impure creature, perhaps the dirtiest, and regards her as a synonym for the temptress. 'The Fathers of the Church and the preachers did not cease to utter their thunders against woman, disparaging her, and abusing her as the impure creature, almost devilish.' (C.J.M. Lectourneau, *The Evolution of Marriage and of the Family*, New York, 1911, p. 205.) 'In the first few centuries of the Christian era the Western world was inundated with some very remarkable notions about women which came to them from the hills of Tibet ... Women were told, with all the weight of a sacred authority, that they should be ashamed of the thought that they were women, and should live in continual penance on account of the curses their sex had brought into the world. The very phrases of Manu (1st Century BC author of Hindu religious law) used against women were: "the door of hell, the personification of sin." Some even went so far as to suggest that their bodies were of diabolic origin ...'[8]

Similarly, the balanced Islamic outlook on sex, recognising it as a natural, desirable biological urge in men and women, is in sharp contrast to the Christian stance on the subject:

> In Christian teaching ... marriage is not the greatest human good; it may have to be foregone (as in the vow of celibacy in monasticism) in order to do the will of God. There is also a more negative strain of thought in Christianity, going back to Augustine's view that the original sin was transmitted through the sexual act ... Associated with this is an ambivalent attitude to women, connected with the image of Eve the temptress.[9]

Another regulation related to fasting discussed in the passage states that one should not have sexual relations with one's wife during one's devotional retreat in a mosque. This thus reinforces the point that life should be lived in total accordance with Allah's commands. The elaborate exercise of a month-long fast trains man in the same way: namely, by obeying Allah unquestioningly, of surrendering himself fully to Him even in such matters of his daily life as food, drink and sex, and of equipping himself with God-consciousness, self-restraint and self-discipline. This represents the essence of fasting and holds the key to man's success in both worlds.

Related Qur'ānic passages for self-study

- al-Dukhān 44:1-8
- al-Qadr 97:1-5

References

1. *Chambers Dictionary of Beliefs and Religions*, op. cit., p. 172.
2. Daryābādī, *The Glorious Qur'ān*, op. cit., p. 62.
3. *Chambers Dictionary of Beliefs and Religions*, op. cit., p. 172.
4. *The Bible*, op. cit., p. 402.
5. Daryābādī, *The Glorious Qur'ān*, op. cit., p. 62.
6. *Chambers Dictionary of Beliefs and Religions*, op. cit., pp. 463-464.
7. Daryābādī, *The Glorious Qur'ān*, op. cit., p. 65.
8. Ibid.
9. *Chambers Dictionary of Beliefs and Religions*, op. cit., p. 100.

11

Charity (*Ṣadaqah* and *Zakāh*)

Virtue is not in this that you turn your faces to the east and the west, but it is virtue

to believe in Allah, and the Last Day and the angels and the Book and the Messengers;

to give of your belongings, out of love for Allah, to your kin, orphans and the needy, the wayfarer, those who ask, and for freeing necks;

to establish Prayer, and give Zakāh*;*

to fulfil the promises you have made, to be patient in adversity and pain, and in time of violence.

(al-Baqarah 2:177)

The obligatory alms are for

the poor, the needy, and the agents employed for it, those whose hearts are to be reconciled, freeing necks, helping those burdened with debt, and expenditure in the way of Allah, and the wayfarer. This is an obligation from Allah, the All-Knowing, the All-Wise.

(al-Tawbah 9:60)

APART from elucidating the concept of charity and listing its beneficiaries, the above passages stand out as a comprehensive statement of Islam as a faith and its practices. For these provide a synoptic account of the articles of faith in Islam. Pride of place goes to belief in Allah, the One True God. Next to it is the affirmation of the doctrine of the Hereafter with its resultant divine reckoning. One is obliged also to profess faith in the angels, Scriptures and messengers. Since Islam prescribes strict monotheism, it grants no space for polytheism, atheism or any "ism" which runs counter to its basic tenets. The monotheistic tenor of Islam categorically demands that one should turn only and wholly to Allah, the supreme Lord.

Virtue or piety consists in obeying and serving Allah unquestioningly. Faith or virtue is not to be equated with the observance of some soulless ritual or outward religiosity. To illustrate this truth, pointed reference is made in the passage to the direction of worship. Notwithstanding its importance in faith, the idea of facing a particular direction while worshipping derives its sanctity only from Allah's command. Until Allah asked Muslims to take the Ka'bah in Makkah as the direction of worship Muslims used to offer their Prayers facing Jerusalem. No sooner did Allah replace this, than the Muslims faithfully followed His command changing their direction of worship. What really matters in faith is the readiness to obey Him. That Islam places a premium on man's self-surrender to Allah, rather than mere form or hollow ritual also comes out in the following Qur'ānic pronouncements:

And it is no virtue that you enter your houses by their back doors, but the virtue is to fear Allah.

(al-Baqarah 2:189)

It is neither their flesh (of sacrificial animals) nor their blood that reaches Allah, but it is your piety that reaches Him.

(al-Ḥajj 22:37)

In Islam the concept of virtue is closely linked with professing firm belief in the articles of faith, with performing religious duties such as Prayer and fasting and with treating fairly the men and women with whom one comes into contact. The description of Islamic faith and practice in the passage may be better appreciated by reading it together with those that follow:

> *O Believers! Believe in Allah and His Messengers and the Book He has sent down to His Messenger, and the Book He sent down earlier. And he who disbelieves in Allah, His angels, His Books, His Messengers and the Last Day, has strayed far away.*
>
> (al-Nisā' 4:136)
>
> *The believers affirm faith in Allah, His angels, His Books and His Messengers, saying: We do not discriminate against any of His Messengers. And they say: We hear and obey. We seek Your forgiveness, our Lord! And to You is our return.*
>
> (al-Baqarah 2:285)

The opening part of the passage, besides defining Islamic faith and virtue, strikes at the roots of polytheistic notions about direction – worshipping which had even gained currency among the Christians:

> Both directions – the east and the west – have been held sacred by many pagan nations. In Greek religion, deities were classified as Olympian and Chthonian. The east was the abode of the Olympian gods and the direction to which their temples looked and their worshippers turned when sacrificing to them, "while the west was the direction which the worshippers of Chthonian gods faced." (*Dictionary of the Bible,* vol. 5, p. 134). According to the Hindus, the direction of south-east was sacred to Manu and the performances of *Shuddha* faced it during the ceremony. (*Encyclopaedia of Religion and Ethics,* vol. 12, p. 618). It was the belief of the early Church that evil entered from the north ... There are a few early churches in Shopshire and the border counties that are without their north door ... Islamic worship is not directed towards any direction as such – east, west, north, or south – but towards a particular House, on whatever side of the worshipper it may happen to be.[1]

Amid the good deeds which constitute the bedrock of the Islamic value system, the first and foremost is the practice of charity, as is evident from the above Qur'ānic passage. In the other passage, charity is prescribed as a religious duty obligatory on all Muslims. Known as *zakāh* in Islamic terminology, it stands for "the mandatory payment of one's valuables, provided these are of a certain amount and have been in possession for one lunar year. The amount varies according to the nature and quantum of valuables, but generally it is 2.5% or one-fortieth of the total value".[2]

Central to the Islamic concept of both charity and *zakāh* is the same spirit of total surrender and obedience to Allah, which we noted with regard to the direction of worship. Notwithstanding his natural attachment to his assets, man should give out of this as directed by Allah, and out of love for and devotion to Him. The Qur'ān presses home this important point emphatically, and articulates this in a variety of ways. Take the following as illustrative:

> *And they (the believers) feed, for love of Allah, the needy the orphans and the captive, saying: We feed you only for the sake of Allah. We do not want any return or thanks from you.*
>
> (al-Insān 76:8-9)

In Islam, giving one's dearest possessions to the needy serves as a believer's test of faith:

> *You cannot attain piety unless you spend of what you love. And Allah knows what you spend.*
>
> (Āl 'Imrān 3:92)

Rather, one should give in charity, even if one needs it oneself. This glorious example was set by the *Anṣār* (Madinan Muslims of the Prophet Muḥammad's day) who generously offered all that they had to the Muslim migrants from Makkah, who had to leave their hearth and home in order to escape the unbelieving Quraysh's persecution. The Qur'ān praises their noble gesture:

They prefer them above themselves, even though there was want among them. And whoever is protected against the greed of the self, he is blessed.

(al-Ḥashr 59:9)

The Islamic concept of charity is premised on the virtues of self restraint, self-discipline and utmost devotion to Allah. As any other human being, a Muslim loves to spend his money as he likes. Similarly, he realises how precious his hard-earned money is. Yet, out of love for Allah and acting in the spirit of self-discipline, ingrained in him by Islam, he exercises self-control. Cheerfully he spends money in accordance with Allah's directives. So doing, he ungrudgingly places divine rulings above his interests. This Islamic stance is part of its broader scheme of things, according to which man is only a trustee, with some possessions placed under his charge such as his body, his physical and intellectual faculties and potentials and his earnings. On the Day of Judgement he will be asked to render an account as to how he spent what was granted to him. Guided by these beliefs, Muslims make a point of spending as the Qur'ān directs them. Islam being a practical way has clearly spelled out the specific heads of account on which man should spend. As regards the recipients of charity and *zakāh*, the Qur'ān has identified the following:

1. One's kith and kin figure at the top of the list of persons to whom charity should be given. This directive underscores the divine wisdom behind forging, maintaining and strengthening the social fabric. One should first help one's close relatives, if they need it. This goes a long way towards cementing social ties and eliminating jealousy. Such help also has a multiplier effect, encompassing all the needy members of the community. If every rich person extends financial assistance to his near relatives, its overall effect is a marked decrease in economic disparity among the members of the community. More importantly, it promotes bonds of fraternity and mutual help and support.

2. The orphans being weak and vulnerable members of the community are mentioned in particular. Once again, this directive

underscores Islam's concern for the weaker, underprivileged sections of society. At another place, the Qur'ān exhorts that generous help be extended to the orphans:

> *They ask you concerning orphans. Say: The best thing to do is what is for their good. If you mix with them, they are your brethren. Allah knows the man who means mischief from the man who means good. And had Allah so willed, He could have afflicted you.*
>
> (al-Baqarah 2:220)

3. In similar vein is the directive for providing relief to the needy. According to the Prophet, included in this category "are those who cannot make both ends meet, who face acute hardship and yet whose sense of self-respect prevents them from asking for aid from others and whose outward demeanour fails to create the impression that they are deserving of help".[3]

4. As to the needy, the term "applies to those who depend for their subsistence on others. The word includes all those who are needy, regardless of whether they are so because of factors such as physical disability or old age. It also includes those who have become needy owing to accidental circumstances which have rendered them orphans, widows, unemployed or temporarily disabled".[4]

5. Slavery was an integral part of not only seventh centry Arabia, but also of the entire world. Islam effectively introduced and enforced a number of measures for ameliorating the plight of slaves. As part of its drive for their emancipation, the Qur'ān directed that charity money be spent on securing their release. This could be done in two ways: first, if a slave entered into an agreement with his master that he would be granted freedom on payment of a specified sum of money, financial assistance may be provided to him to make the payment and thus secure his freedom. Second, *zakāh* funds may be used to buy slaves with the intention of setting them free.[5]

6. In addition to helping various categories of people in need through *zakāh*, as detailed above, a strategic purpose is also served by offering financial assistance to calm those who are actively engaged in hostile activities against Islam, or to win over the support of those who are in the unbelievers' camp.[6] Payments were made to persons belonging to this category in the Prophet's day and this strategy paid rich dividends. There is, however, some disagreement among jurisprudents about whether this category is still valid, after the Prophet's passing away and since Islam is deeply entrenched.

7. Those in debt and suffering from poverty on this account also deserve to be helped out of *zakāh* and charity funds. It is part of the broader economic system of Islam that every member of the community should be self-supporting and contribute to public welfare. Help should therefore be extended to those in debt so that they can start earning money with peace of mind. It relieves them of the economic, psychological and emotional crisis affecting them.

8. Another wide-ranging category for utilising *zakāh* and charity money is what the Qur'ān terms as "in the way of Allah". Some scholars interpret this specifically in terms of helping financially those engaged in *jihād*; others maintain that help be granted to poor students of the Islamic religious institutions, those dependant and preaching Islam through their academic work, needy pilgrims and for all good deeds. After all, the objective is to win Allah's pleasure.

9. In recognition of the special circumstances faced by travellers, the Qur'ān directs that help be rendered to them, if they need it during their journey. For example, they may unexpectedly fall short of money, far away from home. Refugees may also be included in this category. At one end of the scale, Islam encourages that financial assistance be provided to one's needy kith and kin and the poor locally and at the other, it urges help for strangers on a journey. The sweep of *zakāh* beneficiaries is thus all-encompassing.

10. Islam aims at institutionalising *zakāh*. Accordingly, it provides extensive guidance as to who should be helped. For facilitating the collection and distribution of *zakāh* it directs that agents be appointed and their remuneration be paid out of *zakāh* funds.

Taken together, the Islamic concept of *zakāh* and charity is remarkably elaborate, catering for the economic and social concerns of the community.

Some of its remarkable features, as enumerated by Mushfiqur Rahman, are:

- It reminds man that all his assets belong in the real sense to Allah alone. It is significant that in its directives to pay *zakāh*, the Qur'ān uses the phrase: "and give of what Allah has given you". One is asked to give only a small portion of all that is granted one by Allah.
- It purifies and ennobles the soul, purging as it does one's heart of selfishness, greed, meanness, miserliness and love of money. This, in turn, renders one as a better human being, a valuable member of the community and Allah's devout servant.
- It instructs one in large-heartedness and generosity. One develops the regular habit of helping the poor and needy.
- It instils in one the virtues of compassion, mercy, tenderness and genuine concern for one's fellow human beings. Needless to add, it contributes much to better, pleasant social relations.
- *Zakāh* and charity are an excellent mode of expressing thanks to Allah for His numerous favours. Imām Ghazālī makes a fine point in his observation that one offers thanks to Allah for the bounties of creation by saying prayers and one displays thanks to Him for material bounties by paying *zakāh*.
- *Zakāh* is an effective means for overcoming the love of this-worldly things, which in turn, boosts one spiritually. Charity helps man transcend materialism and attain spiritual joy. The nature of material attraction is such that once an object is acquired, the goal is then set to acquire another object that will bring new satisfaction. This is

an endless cycle. *Zakāh* helps one break this cycle, for when paying *Zakāh* one spends money that brings one no material benefit.

- One's generous charity and regular payment of *zakāh* has a fulfilling and rewarding effect, which prompts one to engage more in acts of worship. This also boosts one's self-esteem and helps one grow as a better individual.[7]

- *Zakāh* not only purifies wealth, it also ennobles the heart and mind of one who pays it cheerfully. For it gives one spiritual satisfaction for having discharged one's duty towards Allah and for having contributed one's bit towards the welfare of fellow human beings. This point is to the fore in the following *ḥadith*:

  Pay *zakāh* out of your property, for truly it is a purifier which purifies you, and be kind to your relatives, and acknowledge the rights of the poor, neighbours, and beggars.

- Allah has promised to bless him who makes a point of spending in His way:

  Allah enlarges and restricts the sustenance to such of His servants as He pleases, and what you spend in the least (in His cause) He replaces it, for He is the best of providers.

  (Saba' 34:39)[8]

The Prophet reiterates the same truth in his remark that wealth does not decrease on account of charity.

- Throughout, the Qur'ān defines the believer as the one who regularly practises charity and pays *zakāh*:

  And the believing men and women are friends to one another; they enjoin good and forbid evil, and establish prayer and pay zakāh. *They obey Allah and His Messenger. Allah will surely show mercy to them. Allah is Mighty, All-Wise.*

  (al-Tawbah 9:71)

  And worship Allah, and do not join anyone with Him, and show kindness to parents, relatives, orphans, the needy, the near neighbour and the distant neighbour, the companion by your side, the wayfarer, and those whom your right hands possess.

(al-Nisā' 4:36)

You cannot attain virtue unless you spend of what you love. And whatever you spend, Allah knows it.

(Āl 'Imrān 3:92)

They ask you (O Prophet) as to how they should spend. Say: Whatever you spend of wealth, let it be for parents, relatives, orphans, the needy and the wayfarer. And whatever good you do, Allah knows it.

(al-Baqarah 2:215)

In as many as 82 places the Qur'ān mentions *zakāh* together with Prayer as a religious duty. For such descriptions it is helpful to study, at least, the following passages: al-Tawbah 9:60; al-Isrā' 17:26 al-Aḥzāb 33:33 and al-Muzzammil 73:20.

It is perhaps needless to add that since Muslims pay *zakāh* as a religious obligation, it is meant essentially for deserving Muslims. Nonetheless, all poor people, irrespective of their faith, sect, caste or colour should be helped out of charity funds. It must, however, be ensured that these non-Muslims are not actively engaged in fighting against Islam and Muslims. Both the Qur'ān and many *aḥādīth* exhort that only the poor be helped. They draw no distinction between Muslims and non-Muslims on this count. Nor is it forbidden to render financial help to a sinful Muslim.

The extensive guidance about the recipients of charity in the Qur'ānic passage is rounded off with the command to offer prayers and pay *zakāh* regularly. It is followed by the instructions regarding transactions and interactions with fellow human beings. One's conduct, the Qur'ān stresses, should be characterised by these two important traits – to fulfil one's promise and to display self-restraint and perseverance. As to the former, it lies at the core of man's social and economic life. Accordingly it is emphasised that one should honour one's contract. At another level, this directive reminds man to be faithful to his covenant with his Creator and supreme Lord, Allah in obediently following the way shown by Him. The command to offer prayers and paying *zakāh*, as noted above, stems from the same. In asking man to be true to his word the Qur'ān states the main requirements of faith, with the threefold division of i) Islamic belief, ii) Islamic devotion, and iii) the Islamic code of social and moral duty.[8]

Equally important is the virtue of self-restraint and perseverance which should be displayed in adversity, especially when facing financial problems and lack of resources for sustenance; in affliction when one is struck by disease and emotional distress; and during times of violence against the enemies of faith. For a believer these are testing times for his excellent conduct, for his reposing his trust in Allah and for his surrender to Allah's will. One who rises to the occasion proves his faith as true, which is an unmistakable sign of piety. Needless to say, piety is the highest honour imaginable for man. Once again, it is the spirit of piety which prompts one to give generously in charity and to pay *zakāh* cheerfully and regularly. The Qur'ānic concept of charity is anchored on piety and hence its mention in this context.

Like Prayer and fasting, *zakāh* was prescribed as a religious duty for earlier believing communities. This point is specifically made in several Qur'ānic passages such as Maryam 19:30-31 and 54-55 and al-Anbiyā' 21:73. The Qur'ān delivers a dire warning against those who do not pay *zakāh*:

> ***And those who hoard up gold and silver and do not spend them in the way of Allah, warn them of grievous torment on the Day of Judgement. On the Day when (the hoarded wealth) shall be heated in Hellfire and their foreheads, their sides and their backs shall be branded with it (and it would be said to them): "This is what you hoarded up for yourselves. So taste now what you used to hoard up."***
>
> (al-Tawbah 9:34-35)

It is in man's own interest to grasp and practise the Islamic concept of charity and *zakāh*.

Related Qur'ānic passages for self-study

- al-Baqarah 2:110
- al-Tawbah 9:103
- Fāṭir 35:29-30
- al-Ma'ārij 70:24-25
- al-Mā'ūn 107:1-7

References

1. Daryābādī, *The Glorious Qur'ān*, op. cit., p. 60.
2. Ibid., p. 16.
3. Mawdūdī, *Towards Understanding the Qur'ān*, op. cit., vol. III, p. 221.
4. Ibid.
5. Ibid., p. 224.
6. Ibid., p. 222.
7. Some of the material on the features of *zakāh* is taken from Mushfiqur Rahman, *Zakāh Calculation: Primarily Based on Fiqh uz-Zakāt by Yūsuf Qaraḍāwī*, Leicester, UK, Islamic Foundation, 2003, pp. 14-17. This is a helpful guide on *zakāh*, particularly for Muslims in the West.
8. Daryābādī, *The Glorious Qur'ān*, op. cit., p. 61.

12

Pilgrimage (*Ḥajj*)

Recall When we gave to Abraham the site of the Sacred House (the Ka'bah), directing him: Do not associate anyone with Me in worship, and keep My House pure for those who walk around it, those who prostrate (in worship). And proclaim the Pilgrimage among mankind. They shall come to you on foot and mounted on lean camels from every distant point. That they witness the benefits to them and may mention the name of Allah on the appointed days over the cattle He has provided them. So eat of it and feed the hungry poor. Then let them tidy themselves up, fulfill their vows and circumambulate the Ancient House.

(al-Ḥajj 22:26-29)

And fulfil Ḥajj *and* 'Umrah *for Allah ... And fear Allah, and know that Allah is strict in punishment. For* Ḥajj *are the months well known. So whoever undertakes that duty, let there be no obscenity, wickedness or wrangling during* Ḥajj. *And whatever good you do, Allah surely knows it. And take provision for the journey. Surely the best provision is piety. And fear Me, O men of understanding! It is no fault in you, if you seek the bounty of your Lord (during* Ḥajj*). Then when you pour down from 'Arafāt, celebrate the praises of Allah at the sacred monument. Celebrate His praises as He has guided you, and you were astray before this. Then pass on a* *quick pace from the place other people pass on, and ask for Allah's forgiveness. Allah is All-Forgiving, All-Merciful. And when you have completed your rites, celebrate the praises of Allah, as you used to celebrate the praises of your fathers, or with far more heart and soul ... Celebrate the praises of Allah on the appointed days. Then whoso hastens to leave in two days, there is no blame on him, and whoso stays on, there is no blame on him, if his aim is to do right. And fear Allah and know that you will be gathered unto Him.*

(al-Baqarah 2:196-200 and 203)

PILGRIMAGE, an important religious duty in Islam, is described at length in the Qur'ān, as is evident from the two passages quoted above. Some of the points addressed include: the House of Allah (the Ka'bah) and its credentials, how the Prophet Abraham (peace and blessings be upon him) proclaimed Pilgrimage and the response to it down the ages, the benefits of pilgrimage, and how it represents the essence of all other acts of devotional worship in Islam, especially the spirit of piety and surrender to Allah pervading every aspect of pilgrimage.

The Qur'ānic passage opens with placing pilgrimage in its historical context. At Allah's directive and at the site identified by Him, the Prophet Abraham constructed the Ka'bah, the House of Allah, and hence its special, hallowed status. Nonetheless, this account is immediately followed by a condemnation of polytheism in any form. It appears that the above note is intended to clarify beyond any shadow of doubt that the Ka'bah owes its exalted position only in view of its close association with Allah. The structure of the Ka'bah itself has no sanctity of its own. It is Allah the One True God, not the Ka'bah, which is to be worshipped. As for keeping it clean and pure, the directive has both

> a literal and a figurative sense, clear of all material and spiritual filth – for all true worshippers of the One Universal God. Furthermore, the House, itself, is not to be taken as an object of worship: it is simply a place for worshipping the One.[1]

After the Prophet Abraham (pbuh) had constructed the Ka'bah and ensured that only the One True God would be worshipped there, Allah directed him to issue a general proclamation, asking people to visit the Ka'bah. Daryābādī pertinently draws attention to the fact that this proclamation was made

> thousands of years ago, before the era of the press, the post, the telegraph, the wireless, the radio, television and other such paraphernalia of modern publicity and propaganda that mankind has been responding to during all these centuries, by performing the pilgrimage in their tens and hundreds of thousands every year![2]

Amid the various acts of worship prescribed in Islam, *Ḥajj* stands out above others in many respects. That the performance of *Ḥajj* provides an opportunity to pilgrims "to witness the benefits to them" is a special feature of *Ḥajj*. The above point is made in Allah's directive, asking mankind to perform *Ḥajj*:

> *And proclaim the Pilgrimage among mankind. They shall come to you on foot and mounted on lean camels from every distant point. That they may witness the benefits to them and may mention the name of Allah on the appointed days.*
>
> (al-Ḥajj 22:27-28)

The benefits accruing to pilgrims are numerous and varied – religious, financial, social, political and intellectual. Down the millennia pilgrims have witnessed these benefits. This truth comes out at its sharpest in their numerous narratives and travelogues. There is hardly a pilgrim who returns home without experiencing some of these benefits. It is commonplace that each act of worship has its own benefits. However, the benefits gained from *Ḥajj* are, relatively speaking, much more palpable and pronounced, observable to both pilgrims and non-pilgrims.

Winning Allah's pleasure is, of course, its greatest benefit, which cannot be matched by any other gain imaginable. Accordingly, the Prophet Muḥammad (peace and blessings be upon him) clarified that on accomplishing *Ḥajj* a pilgrim is akin to a new-born baby in being pure and sinless.

Amazingly enough, the moment one intends to perform *Ḥajj*, a sea-change sets in one's mindset, psychological make-up; in sum, on one's entire outlook on life and benefits start pouring in immediately. For *Ḥajj* represents, so to speak, the pervading spirit of all the prescribed acts of worship in Islam. The constant mention and remembrance of Allah and chanting certain formulae during *Ḥajj* are the unmistakable hallmarks of *dhikr* (remembrance of Allah) which permeate *Ḥajj*. This mention of Allah at appointed times during the course of *Ḥajj* also captures the spirit of *ṣalāh*, which is incorporated into *Ḥajj*. A set of certain restrictions, forbidding pilgrims the use of otherwise perfectly lawful and wholesome things during the state of *iḥrām*, reminds one readily of the prohibitions placed on one during the month-long fasting during Ramaḍān. Taken in this sense, *Ḥajj* incorporates features which are special to fasting. The journey undertaken to perform *Ḥajj*, often entailing inconvenience and suffering, re-enacts the essential component of the *Hijrah* (migrating in the cause of Allah). For in both of these acts of worship one willingly undergoes discomfort and emotional, material and monetary loss for the sake of Allah. By the same token, some features specific to *Jihād* (striving in Allah's cause) also characterise *Ḥajj* as the pilgrim makes sacrifices related to both his body and belongings. It goes without saying that to perform *Ḥajj* the pilgrim incurs expenses. This reinforces the spirit underlying *zakāh* that man is only a trustee over the material resources endowed on him by Allah and that he should spend in consonance with Allah's directives. Animal sacrifice, another prescribed act of worship in Islam, happens to be one of the major rites of *Ḥajj* itself. Viewed thus, *Ḥajj* displays the quintessence of all the main acts of worship in Islam – prayer, fasting, *zakāh*, *hijrah*, *jihād* and *ḍhikr*. One may therefore, maintain that this single act of worship – *Ḥajj* – renews in one the spirit pervading several acts of worship which is a benefit beyond all measure.

Furthermore, each rite of *Ḥajj* is characterised by many benefits which have both functional and catalytic value. The donning of *iḥrām* makes one realise paradoxically both the importance and worthlessness of clothes, of which one is habitual since birth. Clothes invest one with identity – individual, social and ethnic. Cloth is doubtless one of Allah's major bounties bestowed on man. At Allah's command however, one stops using one's traditional clothes during the state of *iḥrām*. This amounts, in a sense, to removing an artificial barrier to the unity of mankind. Pilgrims dressed in frugal *iḥrām* display the essential sameness of mankind, cutting across distinctions of social class, financial status and ethnic origin. The strong individuality exhibited, rather reinforced by one's preferential clothes, is instantly replaced by the awe-inspiring unity of mankind, with each one of the millions of pilgrims, assembled every year during the *Ḥajj* period, represented only as an obedient servant of Allah. *Iḥrām* thus instructs one in the ideal of mankind's unity, which has assumed greater importance and relevance in today's conflict-riven and disunited world. More importantly, the donning of *iḥrām* places certain restrictions on one, ranging from refraining from sexual relations with one's wife to hunting or wearing perfume, etc. This further infuses and strengthens a spirit of self-restraint. A pilgrim in *iḥrām* is not allowed to kill even an insect. He is not to indulge in fighting, obscenity or evil. Avoiding aggression and controlling animal instincts are thus the benefits arising out of donning *iḥrām*.

Talbīyah (chanting during *Ḥajj*) is of immense benefit for the pilgrim. At one level, it facilitates the bonding between man and Allah, between the creature and the Creator. At another, it helps one discover one's true self – of wholesale surrender to the Supreme Lord. One's sense of proximity with Allah is further heightened by the sacred locale of *Ḥajj* sites. The House of Allah and other structures and places with thousands of years of rich history and their association with such august figures as Allah's Messengers, from the Prophets Abraham and Muḥammad (peace and blessings be upon them) to the latter's Companions, make one inhale and imbibe the sense of the sacred and sublimate one spiritually and emotionally. At the same time, this grand setting humbles one, making one all the more conscious of one's failings and lapses in being true and faithful to one's covenant with one's Lord. Psychologically and morally it brings such benefits which a pilgrim treasures throughout his life. The *talbīyah* and *Ḥajj*-setting help a pilgrim release and ennoble his feelings, especially towards his Creator and Lord. The sense of liberation and purgation is enhanced by the immediate environment and constant mention of Allah which form part of *Ḥajj*.

The visit to *Ḥaram* (the sacred mosque) further heightens the sense of the hallowed and the sacred. It is innate in human nature to exteriorise, objectify and perceive the sacred with sense perception. In Islam the sacred is abstract and rightly belongs to the domain of *al-Ghayb* (the Unseen which is beyond the realm of human sense perception). This natural desire on man's part is, nonetheless gratified, to a certain degree, on seeing and going round the House of Allah, a concrete object yet enjoying such a close association with the sacred and the divine. The visit thus has a sublimating and exhilarating effect on the pilgrim's spirit. Needless to add, this benefit is not obtainable anywhere else. Furthermore, the Prophet (peace and blessings be upon him) is on record as saying that a prayer offered within the precincts of the Sacred Mosque is equivalent to one thousand prayers offered in any other mosque. This benefit of *Ḥajj* is too great to be disregarded by any Muslim.

Ṭawāf (going round the Ka'bah) broadens and reinforces one's spiritual benefits. This rite draws the pilgrim into the proximity of the *sanctum sanctorum*. Standing near the Ka'bah, praying at the spot on which the Prophet Abraham (peace and blessings be upon him) had once stood, visiting the Zamzam well and drinking its water, and performing *Sa'ī* between Ṣafā and Marwah all being part of the rites of *Ḥajj*, help the pilgrim re-enact sacred history. This benefit, once again, is special to *Ḥajj*. While regarding himself as part of the grand tradition, the pilgrim gains firm religious conviction. In other words, revivification of faith is one of the great benefits of *Ḥajj*.

During *Ḥajj* the pilgrim imbibes the spiritual experience flowing from the role models of the Prophets Abraham, Ishmael and Muḥammad (peace and blessings be upon them) and of Hager. Each of them represents an illuminating model of wholesale surrender to Allah's will, and of steadfastness, characterised by unflinching resolve and undoubting courage, in following the path prescribed by Him. As the pilgrim observes the places associated with them, he discovers a new level of existence – of surrender to Allah's commands. Taken in this sense, *Ḥajj* stands out as a salvific journey, facilitating the pilgrim's quest for deliverance. For as the pilgrim moves away from his mundane, worldly surroundings and moves on to the open and sacred centre and witnesses first-hand the religious sacra, the doors of his/her perception are cleansed. *Ḥajj* thus has a tremendous transformative effect on the pilgrim, giving a marked measure of coherence, direction and meaning to life.

The standing at 'Arafāt in the company of millions of pilgrims displays the homogenisation of the purpose of the journey and of status. It brings to mind immediately the Grand Assembly before Allah at the end of time when each and every human being will be recompensed in proportion to the record of his/her deeds. At another level, this grand gathering has effectual benefits. For this infuses a strong sense of brotherhood among all the pilgrims. This spectacle of Muslim fraternity cutting across ethnicities, polities, cultures and societies, brings into sharper relief the truth underlying the Qur'ānic assertion about *Ḥajj*. "*And recall when We appointed the House (the Ka'bah) a resort to mankind and a place of security...*" (al-Baqarah 2:125)

Ḥajj embodies the virtuous inclination of the pilgrim's will. It thus serves as an excellent opportunity for ennobling and sublimating one's emotions and responses. As already hinted, *Ḥajj* trains pilgrims in exercising and developing self-restraint. On the way to *Ḥajj*, the pilgrim may be afflicted with troubles which are sent by Allah to test his/her moral mettle. Apart from this, the restrictions flowing from donning *iḥrām* aim at imbuing the pilgrim with a whole array of moral values. Of these, the avoidance of aggression or controlling one's animal instincts is to the fore. The Qur'ānic directives of *Ḥajj* are, significantly enough, tempered with exhortations for self-restraint, something which is pivotal to leading an excellent moral life. Take the following as an instance in point:

> *For* Ḥajj *are the months well known. So whoever undertakes that duty, let there be no obscenity, wickedness or wrangling during* Ḥajj. *And whatever good you do, Allah surely knows it. And take provision for the journey. Surely the best provision is piety.*
>
> (al-Baqarah 2:197)

Likewise, the command for animal sacrifice is followed by the precept denoting charity and fellow feeling … "*Eat some of it and feed the needy and the poor,*" (al-Ḥajj 22:28). All lewdness in word and deed is forbidden. Islam introduced this moral strain at a time when the visit to the Ka'bah during the pre-Islamic period was vitiated by obscenity. The above moral precepts are part of the Islamic code of conduct. These are nonetheless emphasised during *Ḥajj* as part of the pilgrim's moral training. The union of the separate but similar emotional and moral dispositions of pilgrims facilitates this effectual benefit. Through the strong sense of brotherhood and the common bonding of devotion to the same goal as also the moral tenor leaves an indelible imprint on the mind and soul of the pilgrim.

The convergence of pilgrims from all parts of the world, representative of a vast socio-economic catchment area, provides pilgrims with many associational benefits. Acquaintance and social contact with fellow believers revitalizes the sense of community and solidarity and opens up avenues for trade and commerce. Furthermore, the exchange of views on a wide range of issues may be likened to a fresh blood supply in the Muslim polity. More rewarding is the interaction among the *'ulamā'* and jurisprudents from different parts of the world. *Ḥajj* serves as an international gathering of members of various strata of society. It provides an excellent platform for *da'wah*, its strategies, challenges and prospects. Above all, it helps raise the morale of pilgrims as believers.

The benefits of *Ḥajj* are staggering, especially the salvific, associational and effectual ones. Little wonder then that the Qur'ān makes a point of mentioning that Muslims should perform *Ḥajj* so as to witness "the benefits accruing to them". Some of these benefits are recorded graphically in the travelogues of pilgrims of all times and places, especially of new Muslims. Even Orientalists, inimical to Islam, feel compelled to pay a glowing tribute to some of the benefits of *Ḥajj*, as is evident from the following extracts:

> This great international gathering … is an impressive manifestation of the unity of the Muslim world, and serves to keep alive the feeling of brotherhood in Islam. The same

> thought is impressed upon those Muslims who have been unable themselves to make the pilgrimage in that on the very same day in which the sacrifices are being offered outside the city of Mecca, the faithful ... are linked by bonds of sympathy with their more fortunate brethren in the sacred city.[3]

In the same vein is the observation of a distinguished Western historian of Arabia:

> Down through the ages this institution (*Ḥajj*) has continued to serve as the major unifying influence in Islam and the most effective common bond among the diverse believers. It rendered almost every capable Moslem perforce a traveller for once in his lifetime. This socializing influence of such a gathering of the brotherhood of believers from the four quarters of the earth is hard to overestimate. It affords opportunity for Negroes, Berbers, Chinese, Persians, Syrians, Turks, Arabs – rich and poor, high and low, to fraternize and meet together on the common ground of faith.[4]

At the outset of the Qur'ānic verse prescribing *Ḥajj* and *'Umrah* man is clearly told that he should perform these for Allah alone (verse 196 of *Sūrah* al-Baqarah). This assertion stems from the distinct, unmissable strain of pure, unadulterated monotheism in all acts of worship in Islam. There are no doubt sacred sites associated with *Ḥajj*, namely Makkah, 'Arafāt, Muzdalifah and Minā. Yet a pilgrim's attention must be focused all along on Allah. Guided by the same spirit, the pilgrim should perform *Ḥajj* rites in the manner laid down by Him. What follows this is an extensive description of the various norms and rituals of *Ḥajj*. At the conclusion of the verse it is reiterated that God-consciousness and piety should be the pervading spirit of *Ḥajj*. To heighten the effect further, a note of warning is delivered: "*Know that Allah is strict in punishment.*" The message is loud and clear: *Ḥajj* is not to be performed for any worldly consideration, for making a show of one's religiosity or for participating in some religious fair. Rather, it should be characterised by sincerity of purpose and an earnest attempt to seek Allah's pleasure.

Reference has already been made to the restrictions placed on a pilgrim during the state of *iḥrām*, some of which bring to mind the ones observed during fasting in Ramaḍān. In a similar vein is the directive that pilgrims should shun any act smacking of immorality, obscenity, wickedness or wrangling. Since millions of pilgrims converge during *Ḥajj* and have social interaction during the *Ḥajj* period, these teachings for self-abnegation, self-restraint and reinforcing the moral code assume greater relevance and significance. The training thus gained is expected to guide the pilgrim throughout the rest of his life. As a result, both the pilgrim as an individual and the larger community will enjoy peace, order and bliss. Daryābādī aptly remarks:

> The injunction is in striking contrast with the absolutely lewd and obscene rites and practices in the pre-Islamic *Ḥajj*, and also with the conditions prevailing in modern festivals and large religious gatherings of polytheistic people.[5]

The Qur'ān exhorts pilgrims to do good. This is accentuated by the assertion that Allah knows everything. At one level, it brings home the point to them that they cannot escape His punishment for any wrong committed by them. Nor will they be denied any reward due to them. This should infuse into them, piety and keen sense of accountability to Allah. At another level, this is meant to reassure sincere pilgrims that they will be rewarded amply as Allah watches their faithful observance of this duty only for His sake. The next directive for carrying provisions for the *Ḥajj* journey underscores Islam's practical approach to life. Some earlier faith communities mistakenly thought that taking provisions for pilgrimage was tantamount to doubting God's power to provide them with sustenance. They therefore, went on pilgrimage with the erroneous belief that God would sustain them on their way. The Qur'ān stopped this practice, insisting that those proceeding on the *Ḥajj* journey should make the necessary arrangements for themselves. Besides correcting their perspective, the Qur'ān delivers, more importantly, the moral precept that piety is the best provision which should be the overarching concern in performing *Ḥajj*.

Islam does not recognise the division of human activities into such categories as the mundane and the religious, the secular and the divine. Rather, one's entire life should be lived with the objective of winning Allah's pleasure and in consonance with the way prescribed by Him, irrespective of the type of activity in which man is engaged. According to the Islamic worldview, every action which is in line with Islamic teachings is equally praiseworthy, and will carry Allah's reward. This remarkable feature is translated into the permission for pilgrims to carry out business and trade during *Ḥajj*. Like any act of devotional worship, for example, prayer, fasting and *zakāh*, *Ḥajj* too, stands out for its numerous benefits – physical, social, economic, cultural and political. Some of the benefits accruing from *Ḥajj* have been enumerated above. This passage deals in particular with the economic gains of *Ḥajj* which are branded as perfectly legitimate and lawful. Rather, these are described as "the bounty of Allah". Notwithstanding this and other activities, remembrance of Allah and celebration of His praise hold pride of place in the Islamic scheme of Ḥajj. Allah is to be glorified and thanked for His imparting guidance to man. Otherwise, mankind would have groped in the darkness of error and ignorance. For being blessed with such an invaluable favour as His guidance, man, needless to say, stands indebted more to Him than to his biological parents and ancestors. Allah should be remembered constantly during *Ḥajj*, especially in obtaining His pardon and forgiveness. Accordingly, the Qur'ān states that Allah is Most Forgiving and Most Merciful. The passage repeatedly urges man to celebrate Allah's praise during *Ḥajj*. As part of glorifying Him, man should invoke His help and patronage both in this life and the Next. Rather, the Qur'ān instructs man in making this supplication: "*Our Lord! Give us good in the world and give us good in the Hereafter and save us from the punishment of Hellfire.*" (al-Baqarah 2:201) On the import of the above supplication, Daryābādī offers the following insightful observation:

> Note that the object desired and sought in prayer is not the world at all, but good, and good only in whatsoever it may be found – whether in this world or in the Next. Contrast with this the

Christian concept embodied in the reported saying of Christ: "My kingdom is not of this world." (Book of John 18:36)

An ideal prayer, a favourite of the Holy Prophet Muḥammad (peace and blessings be upon him), combining in two brief sentences all the blessings of this world and the Next.[6]

The extensive description of *Ḥajj* in the Qur'ān concludes, significantly enough, with the instruction that deep, all-pervading God-consciousness should underscore one's performance of each and every ritual of *Ḥajj*. Fear of Allah, eventual return to Him and Allah's reckoning in the Hereafter should dominate the pilgrim's heart and mind.

The *Ḥajj* journey symbolises the return to Allah, and hence the emphasis on acting piously and glorifying Allah in the Qur'ānic description of *Ḥajj*.

Related Qur'ānic passages for self-study

- al-Baqarah 2:125-129
- Āl 'Imrān 3:96-97
- Ibrāhīm 14:35-37

References

1. Daryābādī, *The Glorious Qur'ān*, op. cit., p. 600.
2. Ibid., p. 601.
3. T.W. Arnold, *The Islamic Faith*, Lahore, 1910, p. 37.
4. Phillip K. Hitti, *The History of the Arabs*, London, 1948, p. 136.
5. Daryābādī, *The Glorious Qur'ān*, op. cit., p. 72.
6. Ibid., p. 74.

13

Believers

Successful are the Believers. Those who humble themselves in prayers; who avoid vain talk; who are keen on acts of charity; who guard their private parts except with their wives and those who their right hands own. In their case they are free from blame. But those who seek beyond that, they are transgressors. [The Believers are] those who faithfully observe their trusts and covenants, those who guard their prayers. They are the inheritors of Paradise. They shall dwell in it (for ever).

(al-Mu'minūn 23:1-11)

IT goes without saying that the Qur'ān is the Book of guidance *par excellence*, instructing man how to live his life. As part of its grand plan of instruction, the Qur'ān spells out concisely the definition and outstanding features of believers, which are embodied most clearly in verses 1-11 of *Sūrah al-Mu'minūn*. Significantly enough, the *sūrah* itself is entitled al-Mu'minūn (Believers) and it opens with the passage under discussion here. As to the importance and excellence of these particular verses the following *aḥādīth* further clarify the point. It is reported on 'Umar's authority in the *Musnad* of Imām Aḥmad that once after receiving a fresh part of divine revelation, the Prophet Muḥammad (peace and blessings be upon him) made the following supplication in the presence of those Companions sitting around him: "O Lord, Grant us increase and do not afflict us with decrease. Exalt us and do not abase us. Bestow upon us and do not deprive us. Grant us superiority over others and do not deprive us. Grant us superiority over others and do not make others superior to us. Be pleased with us and bless us with Your pleasure." He then added: "I have just now received such verses that whoever acts upon these will go straight to Paradise." He then recited this passage from *Sūrah al-Mu'minūn* which had then been revealed to him. More importantly, the following *ḥadīth* throws ample light on the significance of the passage. On being requested to describe the Prophet's conduct, which would serve as a model for subsequent generations to emulate, 'Ā'ishah, the Prophet's wife, replied that his conduct exemplified what is stated theoretically in the Qur'ān. To illustrate her point further, she recited these verses of *Sūrah al-Mu'minūn*. ("Kitāb al-Tafsīr" in Nasā'ī's *Sunan*.)

On studying these verses one can form a clear idea of the Qur'ānic model of believers. This passage describes both their sound beliefs and right conduct. The first and foremost point is that the Qur'ān accords equal importance to both creed and deed. Both of these should be sound and wedded to the goal of pleasing Allah. Belief which is not supported by right conduct and by the same token, good deeds which are lacking firm belief in the articles of faith prescribed by the Qur'ān, are not acceptable. According to the Qur'ān, a believer is by definition someone who stands out for his good deeds. This amalgam of sound beliefs and right conduct alone ensures success in this world, and more particularly, in the everlasting Afterlife. The Qur'ān assures abiding success to those who display the seven characteristics as outlined in this passage. Another amazing feature of this passage is that it covers the entire gamut of both individual and collective life. Furthermore, it takes into account major social, sexual, moral, economic and spiritual activities. This concise passage thus instructs man in all the important spheres of life, enabling him to profess and practise life as a believer. Implicit in it is also the truth that the profession of Qur'ānic beliefs invests man with excellent conduct and perfect morals and manners. The connection between belief and conduct is logical, rather inevitable. Any flaw in one's conduct betrays some weakness in one's faith. Otherwise, in the scheme of things ordained by Allah, sound beliefs must result in excellent conduct. This explains why the passage opens with the assertion that believers are destined to achieve success. This Qur'ānic proclamation does not hinge on any partisanship or jingoism. It rather states the law of nature that true believers, in view of their perfect conduct, which is expected of them, are bound to attain success.

It also emerges that believers are those who are characterised by, at least, seven features. Belief should imbue them with these seven outstanding traits, observable in their individual and collective life. As already hinted at, these encompass a wide range of human activities. Significantly enough, this account commences and concludes with a pointed reference to *ṣalāh* (prayer). Believers are distinct in terms of their total devotion to prayer. It forms the very pivot of their existence. At one level, prayer signifies their complete surrender to their Creator, their willingness to lead life in accordance with His directives and their concern for their moral and spiritual sustenance and growth. On the singular importance of prayer, the Prophet (peace and blessings be upon him) is on record as saying, as reported by Anas and cited by Aḥmad and Nasā'ī: "Prayer is the joy of my eye."

Not only do believers offer prayer, they do so with the utmost humility. In other words, humbleness towards their Lord and towards fellow human beings is their mark of distinction. Prayer moulds them into better human beings who are considerate and conscientious. The Qur'ānic expression *khushū'* literally means humbleness. This should characterise the believers' prayer, as is emphasised in several *aḥādīth*. Outwardly they should appear humble towards Allah while offering prayers. Moreover, this quality should pervade their hearts. At one level, it underscores their full attention and devotion to various postures within prayer, avoiding any contact with or interest in anything outside prayer while so engaged. In the broader context, however, it points to turning to Allah in all matters of life. Only His pleasure engages them and on a constant and consistent basis. It also ensures their utmost sincerity. It trains them to display total commitment to any task which they undertake. Since only such acts catch their attention which seek to please God, their mindset and their entire way of life are God-oriented. And this is what makes their lives and of others in their company full of peace and cordiality.

As a result of their engagement with prayer, the second feature special to believers is their aversion to anything vain. Whatever does not contribute positively to their moral and spiritual development and to the betterment of the society which they erect, does not evoke their interest. The Qur'ānic expression employed, *laghw*, is pregnant with meaning. Apart from ruling out evil in any form, it strikes a fatal blow to all such pursuits which have only entertainment value. For believers, belief and prayer infuse into them such a sharp and keen sense of responsibility and accountability that nothing vain distracts them. The Qur'ān does not negate the point that the world or human society is or can be altogether free from vanities. Believers, however, make a point of passing it by. Almost the same truth is reiterated in verse 72 of *Sūrah al-Furqān*. In sum, prayer turns them into such decent and God-conscious people that they disregard everything which may distract them from God's way. Avoidance of vain talk and fruitless pursuits is thus their second prominent feature. The importance of this may be appreciated best in the larger social context. If such restraint is observed, it makes social life immensely meaningful and genuinely rewarding.

Another trait of believers is their constant and consistent engagement with acts of charity. This may obviously refer to their hearty payment of the obligatory *zakāh*. Or it may be construed in a general, wider sense of contributing to all such projects which aim at ameliorating the condition of the poor and the underprivileged. Throughout, their main concern is to purify themselves and attain the heights of self-development. Included therein is the development of their morals and manners and the purification of their wealth. In turn, it renders them as devout individuals who care for their fellow human beings and the wider community. Not only do they make a point of cheerfully paying the compulsory *zakāh*, they also participate wholeheartedly in all such projects which bring peace and joy to members of their society. Thus the quality of both individual and collective life is enhanced. A way of life with abundant charity promotes the virtues of hospitality and generosity, creates an atmosphere conducive to cordial social relations and a sense of fraternity and helps ease the tensions arising out of class and financial distinctions. Believers thus create a society which is largely free from inner conflicts and dissensions.

That believers guard their private parts is, once again, a virtue of immense value for both their individual life and for society as a whole. Studied together with the next verse which clarifies that they should only have sexual relations with their wives and the women whom they legitimately possess brings to the fore the healthy Islamic stance on sexual conduct. Islam recognises sex like any other natural function of men and women. It does not prescribe abstinence from sex as a prerequisite for spirituality. Nor does it regard sex as something dirty or shameful. The significance of this Qur'ānic stance comes out more clearly when one compares it with the Christian attitude. In Christianity, sex even within wedlock is seen as an obstacle to achieving salvation. (For details see the Bible: Mt. 22:30 and I Cor. 7:32-34.) Islam strikes a balance in terms of sanctioning sexual ties within marriage on the one hand and on the other, condemning all forms of extra-marital sex as a cardinal sin which incurs God's wrath. In the passage under discussion believers are projected as men and women with this balanced, moderate approach towards sex. Under the sobering influence of Islamic teachings in general and of prayer in particular, believers display exemplary restraint in satisfying their natural sexual urges. In so doing, they do not exceed limits. In essence, a note of moderation permeates the conduct of believers, be it with regard to sex or any other human activity.

The next two traits of believers relate to transactions and their socio-cultural, moral and economic life. Whenever they pledge a trust or are assigned with some responsibility they conduct themselves honourably. Being ever-conscious of their trust to God, it is not surprising to find them so particular about discharging their obligations. Their honesty and fair dealings in monetary and contractual matters contributes to producing and sustaining cordial, friendly social relations, characterised by mutual trust, welfare and sincerity. As a result, the life enjoyed by them is peaceful and fulfilling. Anxiety or the constant threat of betrayal and the rat race in a cut-throat world does not haunt them. On the contrary, their community life is imbued with acts of charity, sexual restraint, good will and fellow-feeling.

Closely related to honouring trusts is the virtue of keeping promises, which also characterises believers. They are ever true to their word to their Creator and to fellow human beings in terms of fulfilling the duties which they owe to God and to their social contacts, starting with familial ties and extending to wider community roles. In so doing, they sacrifice their self-interest. Rather, they lead a life full of self-abnegation and altruism. It goes without saying that such an attitude cements and reinforces strong family and community relations, which become marked by trust, love and understanding. In his sermons addressed to the Companions during his Prophetic career the Prophet Muḥammad (peace and blessings be upon him) made a point of exhorting believers to keep their trusts and promises. He made it plain that one without this virtue cannot be taken as a believer.

This Qur'ānic account, mainly of the conduct of believers in their individual and collective life, is rounded off with a pointed reference to their religious observance. They are particular about offering prayer on time and do not miss it. While at the beginning of the passage humility in prayer is mentioned, the concluding note speaks of punctuality and keenness in offering prayer. They are so diligent in the performance of this duty that they do not miss out any of its components. More significantly, they try their level best to internalise the essence and spirit of prayer in their conduct, as a result of which they grow into perfect human beings. Not only do they observe their religious obligations, they also acquit themselves well of their social role, as a responsible, faithful members of their community.

Believers possessing these traits are promised the inheritance of Paradise, the highest reward imaginable for man. They deserve this in view of their achieving the standard expected of them by God. In essence, the Qur'ānic passage holds out a mirror for us to soul-search and a model to emulate.

Related Qur'ānic passages for self-study

- Āl 'Imrān 3:17
- al-Aḥzāb 33:35
- al-Dhāriyāt 51:16-19
- al-Taḥrīm 66:5
- al-Ma'ārij 70:22-35

14

The Straight Way

Say: "Come, I shall recite what your Lord has forbidden to you":
Do not associate anyone with Him in His divinity.
Be good to your parents.
Do not kill your children for fear of want.
We shall provide for you and for them.
Do not approach shameful deeds, whether open or secret.
Do not take life which Allah has made sacred, except in a just cause.
This He has enjoined upon you so that you may reflect.
And do not approach the property of an orphan except in the best manner until he comes of age.
And give full measure and weight with justice. We do not burden anyone beyond his capacity.
When you speak, be just, even though it be against a near relative.
And fulfil the covenant of Allah. This He has enjoined so that you may remember.
This is My way – the Straight way. Follow it then and do not follow other paths; that will deviate you from His way. This He has enjoined so that you may fear Allah.

(al-An'ām 6:151-153)

THE opening *sūrah* of the Qur'ān, al-Fātiḥah, stands out as man's prayer to Allah. The most important part of this supplication is that man be guided to the Straight Way. According to some scholars, the entire Qur'ān represents the elucidation of this Straight Way. Be that as it may, the passage above neatly spells out what the Straight Way is. For it includes wide-ranging and far-reaching directives, encompassing articles of faith and norms to be observed in everyday life – social, economic and legal. The guidance encapsulated therein aims at alerting man against doing wrong to his Creator, Master and Sustainer, to his parents and children and to fellow human beings, members of his community and society at large. Special mention is also made of the treatment to be meted out to the weaker, underprivileged sections of society. Man's covenant with Allah, his Creator, obliges him to do good and justice to everyone.

Significantly enough, the term of address prefacing the passage is not special to Muslims. Rather, the Prophet Muḥammad (peace and blessings be upon him) is directed to urge everyone to abide by this set of moral precepts which are vital for forging and maintaining a healthy and cordial social life. This underscores the point that the message of Islam is universal in its thrust. It is valid for all mankind, irrespective of time and place.

Since the passage enshrines a definite code of conduct, the style is direct and categorical, asking man to stay away from certain things forbidden by Allah. The range of forbidden items in the passage is, however, much broader than other Qur'ānic passages of similar import which confine themselves to dietary laws. Rather, the acts specified here cover the whole gamut of human activities. More importantly, it is clarified at the outset that these guidelines, coming as these do from the Lord of mankind, must be followed by everyone. Since Allah is the Cherisher and Sustainer, besides providing material resources and sustenance essential for man's survival in this world, He has devised an elaborate code of conduct for man's social, moral, emotional and spiritual existence and welfare. To be precise, this guidance represents the Straight Way and following the same guarantees man's success.

The most outrageous act which the Qur'ān forbids man to do is to associate anyone with Allah in His divinity. Since this is an act of monstrous injustice, it is mentioned at the outset. Man depends on Allah for everything, ranging from the gift of life to every necessity of everyday use. As Allah alone is the One True God, it is the height of injustice, ingratitude and betrayal to invest others with divinity which is exclusive to Allah. Polytheism is the worst form of deviation from the Straight Way prescribed by Allah. Therefore, it is stated that those interested in the Straight Way must first give up polytheism. Seventh-century Arabia, as is recorded in history, was engrossed in idolatry and polytheism. It was an odd twist of irony that hundreds of idols were installed at the Ka'bah in Makkah, the House of Allah meant for worshipping the One True God. It was therefore, all the more necessary to denounce polytheism. Without abandoning polytheism, these Arabs could not perceive or follow the Straight Way. The same holds true in our times as well. Unless we give up our devotion to beings and things other than Allah and dedicate ourselves wholly to Him, we cannot pursue the Straight Way. Monotheism changes man's mindset, prompting him to pledge unquestioning loyalty to Allah, which is essential for following the Straight Way. History testifies that under the able stewardship of the Prophet Muḥammad (peace and blessings be upon him) the Arabs surrendered themselves wholesale to Allah. By dint of such resolve and constancy they scaled new heights of greatness and success in both worlds. At the time the Qur'ān exhorted man to profess and practise belief in the One True God, polytheism was deeply entrenched in the world. Sayyid Mawdūdī ably portrays the scenario of the day:

> Instances of associating others in God's essence are the Christian doctrine of Trinity, the belief of the pagan Arabs that angels are the daughters of God, and the belief of other polytheists in the divine character of their self-styled gods and goddesses, and in some cases, of their royalty. Likewise, a person associates others in the attributes of God when he considers someone other than God to be invested with those attributes which belong exclusively to God.[1]

Apart from this important instruction, couched in forceful language, and related to belief, the Qur'ān passage abounds in guidance regarding all the major aspects of man's life, both individual and collective. The set of directives opens, significantly enough, with an exhortation to treat parents well. In other words, maintaining family relations is the starting point of the social life envisaged by Islam. Parents deserve obedience, respect, love and good treatment in view of their selfless sacrifices and service for their children. Any disrespect towards them amounts to committing a grave injustice. Accordingly, the Qur'ān exhorts man to be good to one's parents. Justice demands that one be grateful to his benefactor. Conversely, ill-treatment of one's benefactor is forbidden. In Islam, the family is the basic unit of society. For ensuring its consolidation and sanctity, it is essential that parents be treated with love and respect. That parents be obeyed is a familiar precept in every faith community and moral system. The Qur'ān, nonetheless, goes a step further in demanding that they be treated in a dignified manner, especially in their old age. Take the following Qur'ānic passages as illustrative of this:

> *Your Lord has decreed that you worship none but Him, and that you be kind to parents. Whether one or both of them attain old age in your life, say not to them a word of contempt nor repel them, but address them in terms of honour. And out of kindness, lower to them the wing of humility, and say: "My Lord! Bestow on them Your mercy as they brought me up in childhood."*
>
> (al-Isrā' 17:23-24)

> *And We have enjoined on man to be good to his parents. In travail upon travail his mother bore him, and in two years was his weaning. Show gratitude to Me and to your parents.*
>
> (Luqmān 31:14)

> *We have enjoined on man kindness to his parents. In pain his mother bore him, and in pain she gave him birth. The carrying of the child to his weaning is a period of thirty months. At length when he reaches the age of full strength and attains forty years, he says: O*

my Lord! Grant me that I may be grateful for Your favour which You have bestowed upon me, and upon both my parents.

(al-Aḥqāf 46:15)

The directive to be good to parents aims at instilling into society the virtues of kindness and selflessness which are the key to a happy, peaceful co-existence among human beings.

Man should adopt a similar selfless attitude regarding his children. Prompted by selfishness, he should not commit such a heinous act as killing his own offspring. This single Qur'ānic command strikes at the roots of several callous manifestations of infanticide. At one level, it prohibits the evil practice on the part of the pagan Arabs of the day who used to bury their daughters alive, apprehending poverty. At another level, it repudiates any state-sponsored family planning project of our own times. For fear of lack of resources lurks behind such projects. The Qur'ān, however, promises divine sustenance for everyone alive and for future generations. Daryābādī aptly remarks on this count: "It is in consonance with this divine guarantee that, contrary to what Malthus and his disciples calculated, the population has not outrun the means of subsistence."[2]

Indulging in indecent and wicked acts, whether privately or publicly, outrages the moral health of society, and hence constitutes a serious wrongdoing and injustice to fellow human beings. For it renders the entire society vulnerable and open to immorality. The young especially are prone to be so afflicted. It perhaps amounts to stating the obvious that a society teeming with vices cannot enjoy peace and happiness. The Qur'ān therefore, makes a point of warning man against acts of indecency. It is worthnoting that man is asked not to even approach a shameful deed, let alone commit one. For shameful deeds are hazardous for the social and moral fabric. The Qur'ānic expression (*faḥshā'*) for shameful deeds is broad in its sweep. Further, the all-inclusive terms of "both open and secret" imply all major sins. Open sins refer to all immoral acts committed publicly while secret sins refer to ill-feelings of jealousy, rancour, lust, ingratitude and lack of trust. Man should be particular about his obligations not only to God, and his parents and children, but also, in equal measure, to members of his society. While someone's mindless acts might destroy the ecological balance and pollute the environment, putting everyone's life at risk, immoral acts, both private and public, pose an equally serious threat to society. The Qur'ān is very particular on safeguarding the moral well-being of all. Therefore, its directives on this issue are incisive and emphatic. The prohibition is all-embracing, covering all forms of obscenity and indecency. In our times while obscenity has regrettably made its way into the arts, the media, culture, and public life, the above Qur'ānic directive needs to be borne in mind and the attention given to it that it deserves.

From the domain of morals and manners the gaze of the Qur'ān turns to the sphere of law and order and public life in general. Respect for life is the cornerstone of Islam. The sensitivity with which Islam handles the issue of the sanctity of human life is amply demonstrated in the following verse:

> *We ordained for the Children of Israel that if anyone slew a person – unless it be for murder or for spreading mischief in the land – it would be as if he slew the whole of mankind and if anyone saved a life, it would be as if he saved the whole of mankind.*
>
> (al-Mā'idah 5:32)

Islam is opposed to all forms of violence and bloodshed. This Qur'ānic directive is as timely today as it was in the lawless society of seventh century marauding Arabs. Taking someone's life is an evidently outrageous wrong and injustice. The Qur'ān therefore categorically forbids it. However, as part of its larger scheme of things governing social life, and more importantly, for meeting the dictates of justice, the Qur'ān qualifies the above prohibition that life cannot be taken, except in just cause. Elsewhere the Qur'ān identifies some cases in which it is lawful to kill those guilty of certain heinous crimes. Sayyid Mawdūdī presents the following synoptic account of the cases in which the otherwise inviolable life forfeits its sanctity:

> The cases mentioned by the Qur'ān are the following: 1) That a man is convicted of deliberate homicide and thus the claim of

> retaliation is established against him. 2) That someone resists the establishment of the true faith so that fighting against him might become necessary. 3) That someone is guilty of spreading disorder in the domain of Islam and strives to overthrow the Islamic order of government.
>
> The two cases mentioned in the *Ḥadīth* are: 1) That a person commits illegitimate sexual intercourse even after marriage. 2) That a Muslim is guilty of apostasy and rebellion against the Muslim body-politic.[3]

Exploitation of the weaker sections of society is a common sight. The Qur'ānic guidance for following the Straight Way covers this aspect of social life as well. For the Qur'ān forbids all forms of usurpation or misappropriation of an orphan's property. The Qur'ān aims at developing such righteousness among man that any wicked thought of taking away an orphan's belongings should not even cross one's mind. For the Qur'ān instructs that the guardian's sole concern should be the protection and betterment of the orphan's interest. He should look after such orphans until they come of age and are in a position to manage their own affairs. The Islamic stance on ensuring the welfare of orphans has elicited the following tribute from a leading Western social scientist:

> One of the most commendable things which one finds in reading the Qur'ān is the solicitude which Muhammad shows for the young, and especially for such as have been deprived of their natural guardians. Again and again, he insists upon kind and just treatment being accorded to children. And working upon his words, the Muhammadan doctors have framed a system of rules concerning the appointment and duties of guardians which is most complete, and extending to the most minute details.[4]

The same Qur'ānic concern for extirpating injustice and for promoting peace and cordial relations in society lies at the core of its other directives for acting with honesty and fairness in business transactions. It goes without saying that fraudulent trade practices make man's life miserable and breed a host of vices which tarnish man's spiritual and moral well-being. Let it be clarified that the directive for giving full measure and weight signifies uprightness on man's part. Included in it, by implication, is the point that man should be conscientious in all that he does. For example, he should perform his duty well and not waste time. Punctuality in duty is as important as precision in weight and measure. As a trader is forbidden from cheating customers, an employee should faithfully serve his employer. The employer too, stands obliged to act fairly towards his employees. The Qur'ānic worldview is all-inclusive. It is not restricted to the performance of obligatory prayers on time in the prescribed manner. Rather, it seeks that the same spirit of devotion to Allah, which permeates one's prayer, should also be reflected in every walk of life, especially in a person's dealings with his fellow human beings. It is not therefore surprising to note that many components of the Straight Way, as embodied in this passage, relate to man's social life, not to devotional theology. As part of the same stance, business practices find mention in clear terms in that these affect all members of society. The Qur'ān insists that these be characterised by fairness, transparency and justice.

After having prescribed this particular code of conduct and exhorted man to abide by it, failing which he will incur Allah's wrath, the Qur'ān comforts man also with an eye on bolstering his morale. It is noteworthy that at the conclusion of these commandments the Qur'ān records the observation that Allah does not burden man beyond his capacity. Gifted with the numerous faculties and potentials granted to him by Allah, man can easily follow all these commands. The Qur'ān has not set man some gigantic tasks, which are beyond his capacity to accomplish. The Prophet Muḥammad (peace and blessings be upon him) and his Companions stood this test and performed admirably what was expected of them. It is not therefore beyond our capacity to emulate them. Implicit in the above assurance is the fact that Allah will condone any lapse on man's part in pursuing the Straight Way, as long as his intention to observe these directives is pious and sincere.

The Qur'ānic exhortation to profess and practise justice at all costs is to the fore, once again, in its directive that man should be fair in his testimony. Evidently this directive is not special to the legal sphere. The thrust is that man should be just and truthful in his social relations. This point emerges on studying the above directive in conjunction with the following verses:

> *O Believers! Stand out firmly for justice, as witnesses to Allah, even as against yourselves, or your parents, or your kin, and whether it be against the rich or the poor. For Allah can best protect both.*
>
> (al-Nisā' 4:135)
>
> *O Believers! Stand out firmly for Allah, as witnesses to fair dealing, and let not the hatred of others to you make you swerve to wrong and depart from justice. Be just. That is next to piety and fearing Allah. For Allah is well-acquainted with all that you do.*
>
> (al-Mā'idah 5:8)

The Qur'ān seeks to impart in man a purity of intent and a fairness and transparency in conduct, which, in turn, facilitates the construction of a society marked by mutual trust and cooperation. It leaves no room for wickedness. True, the Qur'ān places a premium on ties of kinship, urging that one be generous towards one's kith and kin offering them all help and assistance, be it financial, emotional or social. It warns those who sever such ties of divine punishment in the Afterlife. Yet it adopts and prescribes an unrelenting stance towards one's near and dear ones, if justice demands so. Little wonder then that the Qur'ānic command for fair testimony carries the additional note that man should stand for justice, even if it might jeopardise the interests of his near relatives. Only man's unflinching belief in Allah's supreme power equips man with the moral courage and strength to practise such righteousness.

Observance of this code of conduct is branded in the Qur'ān as the fulfillment of man's covenant with Allah. This highly significant statement is ably explained by Sayyid Mawdūdī thus:

> The 'Covenant of Allah' signifies, in the first place, the commitment to God, as well as to human beings, to which man binds himself in His name. It also signifies that covenant

> between man and God, as well as between one human being and another which automatically takes place the moment a person is born onto God's earth and into human society.
>
> For when man enjoys his own existence, makes use of his physical and mental energy, benefits from the means of sustenance and natural resources – in other words, when he benefits from the world created by God and avails himself of the opportunities provided for him by the operation of natural laws – he incurs certain obligations towards God. In the same way, when one derives nourishment and sustenance from the blood of one's mother while in her womb, when one opens one's eyes in a family which is supported by the toil of one's father, when one benefits from the various institutions of human society, one is placed in varying degrees of obligation towards those individuals and institutions.[5]

Islam alone is presented as the Straight Way prescribed by Allah. This categorical statement rules out all other faiths and *isms* as unworthy of man's attention. Notwithstanding its hallmarks of peaceful coexistence among adherents of all faiths, Islam admits no compromise on articles of faith. Islam alone is the truth and it would be a sheer folly to regard all faiths as embodiments of truth. Likewise, the Straight Way stands for the Islamic teachings in their unadulterated form, as conveyed and practised by the Prophet Muḥammad (peace and blessings be upon him) and his Companions. Sectarianism and innovations lie outside the Straight Way, and hence man should shun these. For these are bound to deviate and distract him.

Throughout this Qur'ānic passage, which contains a detailed description of the Straight Way, man is invited to reflect on this code of conduct. The more he analyses this code, the more cognizant he will become about its life-ennobling message. He is also directed to remember these teachings. For in the hurly-burly of life situations or in weak moments, when short-term gains entice, man is liable to deviate from the Straight Way. His constant remembrance of this code will, however, enable him to steadily pursue the Straight Way. More importantly, it will instil into man God-consciousness and piety which are the basic prerequisites for pursuing the Straight Way. It is perhaps needless to say that the above course of action, being devised by Allah, is the only road to success and prosperity in both worlds. By following the Straight Way man is blessed with peace of mind, singleness of purpose and spiritual joy and contentment as also with the eternal rewards of the Afterlife.

Related Qur'ānic passages for self-study

- al-Baqarah 2:83
- al-Nisā' 4:36
- al-A'rāf 7:33
- al-Isrā' 17:23-35
- al-Furqān 25:68
- al-Shu'arā' 26:181-183
- al-Mumtaḥanah 60:12
- al-Muṭaffifīn 83:1-3

References

1. Mawdūdī, *Towards Understanding the Qur'ān*, op. cit., vol. II, p. 290.
2. Daryābādī, *The Glorious Qur'ān*, op. cit., p. 282.
3. Mawdūdī, *Towards Understanding the Qur'ān*, op. cit., vol. II, p. 292.
4. Robert Roberts, *Social Laws of the Quran*, London, 1911, pp. 40-41.
5. Mawdūdī, *Towards Understanding the Qur'ān*, op. cit., vol. II, p. 293.

15

Man's Obligations Towards His Fellow Human Beings

Your Lord has decreed:

i. *Do not worship any but Him.*

ii. *Be kind to your parents, should both or any of them attain old age with you. Do not say to them even a word of contempt. Do not repel them but speak to them in terms of honour. And be humble and kind to them and say: Lord! Have mercy on them as they brought me up when I was small. Your Lord knows best what is in your hearts. If you are righteous, He will forgive those who repent and turn to Him.*

iii. *And give to the near of kin, his due rights, and also to the needy and the wayfarer.*

iv. *Do not squander your wealth wastefully. Those who squander are Satan's brothers, and Satan is ever ungrateful to his Lord.*

v. *And if you turn away from them, awaiting mercy from your Lord which you expect to receive, then speak to them kindly.*

vi. *Do not let your hand be chained to your neck, nor outspread it to its extreme, for you will then be left sitting reproached, destitute.*

Certainly your Lord enlarges the provision for whom He will and measures it out. He is All-Aware and All-Observant of His servant.

vii. *Do not kill your children for fear of want. We provide for them and for you. Surely their killing is a great crime.*

viii. *Do not even approach adultery. It is a shameful deed and an evil way.*

ix. *Do not kill anyone whom Allah has forbidden to kill, except with right. We have granted authority to the next of kin of him who has been killed wrongfully (to claim retribution). So let him not exceed in killing; he shall be helped.*

x. *And do not even go near the property of the orphan, except that it be in the best manner, until he attains maturity.*

xi. *And fulfil the covenant. For you will be questioned regarding the covenant.*

xii. *Give full measure when you measure, and weigh with an even balance. That is fair, and better in consequence.*

xiii. *Do not go after that of which you have no knowledge. Surely the hearing, the sight, the heart, each of them shall be called to account.*

xiv. *Do not walk on earth with insolence. For you cannot cleave the earth. Nor can you reach mountains in height.*

The evil of each of these things is hateful to your Lord.

That is part of the wisdom which your Lord has revealed to you. So do not set up along with Allah another god lest you are cast into Hell, rebuked and rejected.

(al-Isrā' 17:23-39)

APART from performing the prescribed acts of worship, a Muslim has a number of obligations which must be met towards his fellow human beings. Both sets of obligations carry equal importance in Islam and a Muslim is expected to discharge them with sincerity and devotion. This truth comes out sharply in the Qur'ānic passage under study, which opens with the declaration that it is Allah Who has laid down these obligations. These appear in a particular order, the significance of which is worth considering. The code of conduct, outlined in the passage, moves from individual to collective life, from family to community relations at large, from morals and manners to business transactions, and from specific to general guidelines on leading one's life in accordance with Allah's will. The coverage is thus amazingly broad, underscoring as it does Islam's all-embracing worldview. No human activity, which impacts on other human beings, seems to have escaped notice. There are directives for every situation in which man finds himself in daily life. In keeping with Islam's universal message, these precepts are addressed to everyone, irrespective of faith, gender, social standing, financial status, spiritual development or intellectual attainments. Moreover, these obligations are to be discharged, once again, by everyone, without distinction. For example, the directive that one should be kind to one's parents is equally applicable to one's non-Muslim parents or neighbours. Needless to add, it brings into sharper light Islam's moral excellence.

The first and foremost instruction, in line with the Islamic belief system, is to shun polytheism of every hue and variety. Man's good deeds, which are described in the passage, should aim only at winning Allah's pleasure. Islam insists on both sound beliefs and good deeds. Good deeds are not an end in themselves. Rather, they should be exclusively orientated towards obeying the One True God. For in the absence of this belief, one may be prompted by some worldly motive, for example, of gaining fame, in doing what appears as good. This impairs the purity and sincerity of one's good deeds. It is, therefore, imperative that these be performed only for seeking Allah's pleasure. In Islam, it is expected that sound faith will produce good deeds. In recognition of the same, the directive for good deeds is prefaced by the command that one should first embrace sound beliefs.

As to the set of obligations towards one's fellow human beings, let it be realised at the outset that in Islam the family is the most important and sacred unit of life. The moral order hinges on the values governing family life. Islam, therefore, takes every step towards ennobling and fortifying family ties. For children naturally imbibe the values professed and practised by their parents. It is not, therefore, surprising that the Qur'ānic account of obligations opens with the directive that parents should be treated with respect and kindness. On the one hand, this instructs one in the good treatment of the elderly and on the other, it sets a noble example for the young to develop love and respect for their elders. Needless to say, this invests family life and society at large with cordial social relations, sanctity, peace and happiness.

A particular directive is issued that one should be kind to one's parents in their old age, as they need greater help and support at this stage of life. That no word of contempt be used against them reinforces the exhortation to display the utmost love, concern and respect for them. One's behaviour towards them should be characterised by humility. The Qur'ān reminds man, psychologically and emotionally of his total dependence upon his parents during infancy. Out of gratitude for their care and affection one should look after them well in their hour of need. One's realisation of his own helpless condition in infancy should make one all the more humble and grateful towards one's parents. These extensive guidelines are given a cutting edge in so far as they stress the truth that Allah watches man's intention and conduct. This aims at eliminating any negligence in performing one's duty towards one's parents. In the same vein is the reference to Allah's pardon.

Several *aḥādīth* bring into sharper relief this Qur'ānic precept. Once, on being requested to identify the best deed in Allah's reckoning, the Prophet replied: "To offer prayer at its appointed time." He mentioned good treatment of parents as the next best deed. (Bukhārī) It is related on Abū Umāmah's authority that the Prophet stated that one's parents will take one to Paradise or Hell. (Ibn Mājah) What is meant is that one's ultimate end depends largely on one's attitude towards one's parents.

The same spirit of good treatment should be extended to one's kith and kin, the needy in general and travellers. Needless to add, this directive has strong economic, social and moral overtones. Apart from the elaborate law of inheritance allotting shares to the heirs and *zakāh*, Islam also introduced the practice of *ṣadaqah* (alms), *waqf* (charitable trusts) and hospitality for travellers, all of which are imbued with the values of generosity, sympathy and cooperation. These teachings went a long way in creating and sustaining cordial social relations. Islam encourages benevolence towards fellow human beings, especially the needy, which helps control the frustration arising out of economic disparity among the various members of the community. It is worthstating that Islam is not opposed to wealth. Nor does it prescribe monasticism as the preferred way of life. Yet it insists that wealth be shared with close relatives who may need help. Significantly enough, financial help rendered to fellow human beings is described in the above passage as "their due right". Islam thus strikes a remarkable balance between the two extremes of capitalism and communism.

As part of its economic code of conduct, Islam condemns the squandering and abuse of resources put at man's disposal. In Islam man is assigned the role of trustee, enjoying control over what Allah has granted him. It is important then that one uses one's resources prudently. Spending one's money on anything which is sinful amounts to using it wastefully and hence is forbidden. Once again, this economic teaching is permeated with morality. Those guilty of squandering resources are likened to Satan's brothers on the following two counts: i) in squandering their resources they behave like Satan who abuses the faculties granted to him only for disobeying Allah, and ii) squandering betrays ungratefulness to Allah, which is Satan's main personality trait. It is the height of ignominy for man to be branded as one of Satan's party. The Qur'ān employs this strong epithet is order to dissuade man from squandering his wealth. For this strikes a severe blow to the moral fabric of society. Generally speaking, wealth spent wastefully is directed at gambling or at making a show of one's wealth which vitiates social life. That squandering is something evil is effectively brought out by its association with Satan.

Another directive embracing man's financial conduct is that he should treat the needy politely when he is unable to help them. One is not to be blamed, if one cannot help them owing to one's own adverse circumstances. However, what is forbidden is to act harshly and uncharitably towards those in need.

The golden rule governing man's financial conduct is spelled out in the next verse, as is elaborated by Mawdūdī:

> Human beings are required to act with moderation in financial matters. They should neither prevent the flow of wealth out of miserliness, nor should they waste financial resources by irresponsible extravagance. Instead, they should have such an instinctive sense of balance and moderation that they should not shrink from spending when that is genuinely needed, and should abstain from spending when it is not truly needed or is not justified – expenses incurred for show or out of vanity, or on sheer luxury, and for sinful purposes. In fact, every misdirected expense which is made at the expense of genuine needs and beneficial purposes amounts to ingratitude to God for His bounty.[1]

The directive for balance and moderation in financial matters is followed by reiterating the truth that it is Allah Who grants resources to everyone as He wills. Man should not therefore have any grudge against someone with large provisions. Allah has given provisions to man in a measure ordained by Him. He has done so in order to test man, both in prosperity and adversity. He is fully aware of everyone's conduct and will call man to account on the Day of Judgement with reference to his deeds. It is important to clarify that one's wealth or poverty, which is part of Allah's grand plan, is not to be interpreted as a sign of one's proximity or otherwise to Allah. A person blessed with wealth is not necessarily the one with whom Allah is well-pleased. Nor does one's poverty indicate His displeasure. Accordingly, it is stressed that Allah being All-Aware grants sustenance in varying measures to men in accordance with His plan.

Since Allah has promised sustenance for everyone, man should not resort to such ignominious practices as family planning or infanticide out of fear of poverty. For this amounts to interfering with His plan, which is a very serious sin. The Qur'ān forbids this in unambiguous terms, reminding us that Allah, the Provider, will feed everyone. According to Sayyid Mawdūdī:

> This verse totally demolishes the economic basis on which birth control movements have arisen in different periods of human history ... However, according to the provision of the Islamic manifesto, man is required not to waste his energies on the destructive task of reducing the number of mouths that have to be fed ... Human history also bears witness to the fact that economic resources in different parts of the world have increased in proportion to the growth of human population ... Hence, man's amateurish interference in the providential arrangements of God amounts to nothing short of folly.[2]

The focus then shifts from man's economic to social and moral life. As the sex drive in man is a strong natural urge, which must be disciplined in the larger interests of society, mention is first made of living a sexually pure and well-ordered life. Adultery being antithetical to the moral order is singled out at the outset as a cardinal sin. Accordingly, man is directed not to indulge in any act which may draw him closer to committing adultery. This directive speaks volumes about Islam's sensitivity to discipline in sexual life. Islam, unlike some other faiths which glorify asceticism, does not condemn sex. It recognises sex as a natural instinct which should be gratified. Yet it insists that sexual relations should only be within the bounds of wedlock. Since adultery represents sexual anarchy and moral degeneration, striking a severe blow to the social fabric, it is branded as a sin which man must not even approach. To intensifying the effect further, a couple of expressions projecting adultery as something shameful and evil are used. Another point worth noting is that Islam does not recognise consensual sex, pre-marital or post-marital. On this count again, the moral excellence of

Islam comes out sharply in comparison to some faiths which sanction consensual sex – even if it is outside wedlock. In some other faiths there is even a nexus between religion and prostitution and sexual debauchery, as is evident from the following observations recorded in the *Encyclopaedia Britannica*:

> In Egypt, Phoenicia, Assyria, Chaldea, Canaan, and Persia, the worship of Isis, Moloch, Baal, Astrate, Mylitta and other deities consisted of the most extravagant sexual orgies, and the temples were merely centers of vice. In Babylon some degree of prostitution appears to have been even compulsory and imposed upon all women in honour of the goddess, Mylitta. In India the ancient connection between religion and prostitution still survives.[3]

Respect for life is a crucial value in social life. Islam stands for the sanctity of life and brands murder as one of the major sins. It is stressed that life is granted only by Allah and hence no one is authorised to take it away. The only exceptions are five specific cases: retribution against one guilty of deliberate murder; fighting and killing those who are engaged in any uprising against the Islamic system of government; capital punishment for those men or women convicted of unlawful sexual intercourse and capital punishment for those committing apostasy. Nonetheless, the Islamic law of retribution has a way out – paying blood money to the next of kin of someone wrongfully killed. In the larger context, this is a life-giving measure and has a sobering and soothing effect on social life. All Islamic directives are tempered with justice. This point is further endorsed in the directive addressed to the heirs of the victim in so far as they should not transgress the limit in avenging their loss. This directive had radical implications for the immediate addressees, the bedouin Arabs given to revenge killings.

Another precept aimed at ensuring social justice is kindness and sincerity towards orphans. These helpless minors need sincere patrons to protect their interests. The Qur'ān therefore directs that justice and kindness should characterise the guardian's conduct towards orphans.

One should be conscious of one's responsibility and accountability in one's dealings as an orphan's guardian. Throughout the Qur'ān there are several instructions that orphans be treated well by the community in general and by their patrons and guardians in particular. Illustrative of this are verses 2, 3, 6, 8, 10 and 36 of *Sūrah al-Nisā'* and verse 152 of *sūrah al-An'ām*.

This is followed by a general directive that one should be true to one's covenant with everyone, to one's Lord and Creator, Allah and to fellow human beings with whom one has social and financial interactions. All along one should bear in mind one's ultimate accountability on the Day of Judgement. For one will be questioned about fulfilling such obligations. Remarkably, the Qur'ān links everyday life with the Hereafter, investing one's deeds with an unmistakable moral and spiritual tenor. Apart from acts of worship, the routine activities of daily life will be taken into account in the final reckoning and deciding of an individual's fate.

The directive for correct weight and measurement is, once again, stated with a view to inculcating values of honesty, God-consciousness and fairness in both individual and collective life, especially in market transactions. This represents a specific instance of the general precept that one should be faithful to one's covenant. One is obliged to give others what is their due. The most common form of acting on this precept is to give buyers the correct unit of weight and measurement. Again, reference is made to the consequence of this practice in the Hereafter. These points are also brought home energetically and effectively in the following Qur'ānic passage:

> *Woe to those who deal in fraud. Those who, when they take from others, exact full measure. But when they give by measure or weight to men, they give less than is due. Do they not think that they will not be called to account? On the mighty Day, the Day when all mankind will stand before the Lord of the worlds?*
>
> (al-Muṭaffifīn 83:1-6)

Islamic teachings are thus not restricted to prescribing a set of rituals. Rather, these encompass every aspect of life, including business transactions and social interaction. The passage under study abounds in directives which govern one's dealings with one's fellow human beings. Justice, fairness and honesty are emphasised throughout in order to construct a society characterised by trust, love and sincerity.

In conclusion, some general instructions are imparted, placing emphasis on one's role and behaviour in society at large. First, attention is drawn to developing a strong sense of responsibility and accountability. One's physical and mental faculties, as listed in the passage, are like a trust given to one for a certain period of time. One will have to render an extensive account on the Day of Judgement as to how one utilised or abused these faculties and powers. Accordingly, aimlessness in life is condemned at the outset. One should lead a purposive life, geared towards virtues and God-consciousness. This helps one use one's faculties in the best way. This, in turn, protects one against humiliation and punishment on the Day of Reckoning. Islam infuses self-control into man with a view to making collective life happy and peaceful, free from discord which is generally rooted in selfishness.

Pride being a cardinal sin vitiates social relations. For it causes and deepens the divide between people with regard to their social and financial status. It is not, therefore, surprising that the passage under study instructing man in cordial social relations concludes with a strong condemnation of pride and insolence. Man is asked to realise his limitations. Being a creature he cannot surpass his natural limits. He should therefore behave modestly and humbly, which will vastly improve the quality of his own life and of those around him. Being modest and respectful to one's parents is the starting point of Islamic code of conduct outlined in this passage. Significantly, the final piece of advice is, once again, in the same vein, directed at man being humble and kind to everyone with whom he comes into contact. Several *aḥādīth* amplify this Qur'ānic denunciation of pride. Take the following as illustrative. It is related on 'Abdullāh ibn Mas'ūd's authority that the Prophet said: "One with even an iota of arrogance will not be admitted to Paradise." (Muslim) 'Ayāḍ ibn 'Ammār reports that the Prophet said: "Allah has directed that one should act with humility. No one should behave arrogantly towards others. Nor should one wrong anyone." (Muslim)

The social evils referred to in the passage are dubbed as things hateful in Allah's sight. This observation is made in order to evoke man's revulsion towards these. A believer cannot and should not opt for something which is hateful to Allah. The frequent reference to Allah and the Hereafter in this set of directives for everyday life invests the passage with a remarkable blend of this world and the Next and of ordinary human activities and their consequences for man in both worlds. For this and many other features this passage represents the Qur'ānic wisdom which Allah has sent down out of His infinite mercy. It is in man's own interest to greet this invaluable guidance with fervour. Wicked people, who, far from appreciating divine favour, act ungratefully in opposing this message are warned against their utter loss and degradation, for they will be consigned to Hell for their polytheism.

The passage overall thus provides a fair idea of the obligations one is bound to discharge both to Allah and to those in whose midst one lives.

Related Qur'ānic passages for self-study

- al-Nisā' 4:36
- al-An'ām 6:151-152
- al Furqān 25:67
- al-Shu'arā' 26:181-183
- al-Rūm 30:38
- Luqmān 31:14 and 18
- al-Aḥqāf 46:15

References

1. Mawdūdī, *Towards Understanding the Qur'ān*, op. cit., vol. V, p. 37.
2. Ibid., p. 39.
3. *Encyclopaedia Britannica*, vol. 18, p. 58.

16

Treating Parents

And We have commanded man kindness to his parents: with hardship his mother bears him and with hardship she brings him up, and the weaning of him is thirty months, until, when he attains his full strength and attains the age of forty years, he says: "Lord! Grant me the ability that I may give thanks for the favour You have done to me and my parents and that I may act piously such as You may approve. And be gracious to my children. Truly I have turned to You and truly I submit to You (in Islam)."

(al-Aḥqāf 46:15)

And We have commanded man about his parents, his mother bears him in hardship upon hardship, and his weaning is in two years. Give thanks to Me and your parents. Unto Me is the return.

(Luqmān 31:14)

MAN has obligations towards his fellow human beings, but his obligations towards his parents, according to Islam, are of the utmost importance. The Qur'ān mentions this duty, next only to that of serving Allah:

And your Lord has commanded that you should worship no one but Him and show kindness to your parents; and if either or both of them become old, do not say to them "pooh". Do not show any disrespect to them. Speak to them a word of respect. And lower unto them the wings of humility out of kindness and say: Lord! Have mercy on them as they brought me up when young.

(al-Isrā' 17:23-24)

To begin with, the following points are worth noting, as one studies these passages, prescribing how we should treat our parents:

i. That parents are to be treated with kindness and respect features as a divine command in all the above instances. It underscores the tremendous importance attached to this duty in the Islamic scheme of things. It is not some moral precept which one may observe as a dictate of conscience or as a discretionary matter. On the contrary, it is a definite divine command which must be obeyed unquestioningly by everyone and at any cost.

ii. The Qur'ān repeatedly asks man to thank Allah for His numerous favours. Parents alone hold the distinction of being mentioned along with Allah, who deserve to be thanked for their favours. Man is directed to recall with gratitude the favours done to him by his parents. One should constantly bear in mind the exalted rank accorded to parents by the Qur'ān.

Furthermore, besides enacting the command for the good treatment of parents, Allah teaches man the following supplications, which he should make for his parents:

Our Lord! Forgive me and my parents and the believers on the Day of Reckoning.

(Ibrāhīm 14:41)

Lord! Grant me the ability that I may give thanks for the favour You have done to me and my parents ...

(al-Aḥqāf 46:15)

Lord! Forgive me and my parents and him who enters my house as a believer, and all the believing men and women ...

(Nūḥ 71:28)

By making these supplications, love and respect for parents is likely to be ingrained in both mind and heart. Man is thus instructed to regard his parents as an almost inseparable part of his self, as he seeks Allah's forgiveness both for himself and his parents. Islam, thus, ensures that love and respect for parents is infused deeply into man's consciousness. Man should imbibe this truth thoroughly.

iii. Significantly enough, Islam admits no distinction between one's Muslim or non-Muslim parents in treating them well. The parents of many early Muslims in the Prophet's day clung to their ancestral faith out of blind conformity and imitation, and some of them even opposed Islam. Yet these Muslims were directed not to break their family or social ties with their parents. Rather, they were told to treat them well, irrespective of their religious affiliations. The Prophet's noble example bears out this point. It is on record that he always spoke affectionately of his loving uncle, Abū Ṭālib, though the latter refused to embrace Islam, even in the face of the Prophet's repeated and persuasive pleas. The Prophet used to recount gratefully the invaluable patronage and protection extended by Abū Ṭālib and mourned his death, describing it as his irreparable personal loss. The same point comes out unmistakably from the following report, recorded by Bukhārī: "Asmā', Abū Bakr's daughter, sought the Prophet's directive as to how she should treat her polytheistic mother who visited her. The Prophet told her to maintain filial ties with her mother and to look after her well." (Bukhārī)

Other Qur'ānic passages instructing man to treat his parents with love, kindness and respect are verses 83 of al-Baqarah, 36 of al-Nisā', 151 of al-An'ām and 19 of al-Naml. The directive embodied in the above is elucidated in several *aḥādīth*. Take the following for instance:

- The Prophet is on record declaring: "Your Paradise lies under the feet of your mother." (Aḥmad)

- The Prophet spelled out the following as cardinal sins: "To associate partners with Allah, to disobey parents, to commit murder and to give false testimony." (Muslim)
- Once the Prophet exclaimed: "Let him be disgraced!" On being requested to identify the culprit, he clarified: "One who is with his parents in their old age, both or either of them, and yet fails to win a place for himself in Paradise by serving them well." (Muslim)
- That one may discharge one's obligation towards one's parents even after their death is clarified in the following *ḥadīth* reported by Abū Usayd Sā'idi: "Once while we were in the Prophet's company, someone from the tribe of Salamah called on the Prophet and asked him: O Messenger of Allah! Do I owe obligations to my parents even after their death? The latter replied: Yes, you must pray to Allah to favour them with His forgiveness, honour the commitments which your parents made and maintain ties with their relatives and friends." (Abū Dāwūd)

Notwithstanding its emphatic exhortation for kindness towards parents, the Qur'ān makes it plain that they are not to be obeyed if they ask their children to follow a faith other than Islam. Allah alone is to be obeyed in matters of faith, as is evident from the following assertions:

> *If they try to make you associate anyone with Me, of which you have no knowledge, do not obey them.*
>
> (al-'Ankabūt 29:8)

> *If either of them should try to make you associate anyone with Me, of which you have no knowledge, do not obey them, although you may keep company with them honourably in this world. Follow the way of him who turns to Me in repentance.*
>
> (Luqmān 31:15)

Islam adopts a balanced approach regarding one's non-Muslim parents. This issue made its appearance in the early days of Islam. Today, the same problem is faced by new Muslims. On the one hand,

Islam directs a Muslim not to abandon his unbelieving parents. Nor should he/she recant his/her belief in Islam as a result of emotional blackmail from them. That one should adhere steadfastly to Islam once the truth dawns on one is illustrated by Sa'd ibn Mālik's conduct. His acceptance of Islam in response to the Prophet's call was vigorously resented by his polytheistic mother. She refused to take food, demanding that Sa'īd should give up his allegiance to Islam. However, he did not relent and told her plainly that her fasting unto death would not deter him even in the slightest. After a couple of days when her condition worsened and she realised Sa'īd's unwavering commitment to Islam, she recanted her stance and resumed eating and drinking. A Muslim is not to budge an inch in the face of such pressure. Yet a Muslim must make a point of maintaining his social relations with his unbelieving parents. His treatment should be characterised by gentleness and kindness. He should help them financially and emotionally.

In the Qur'ānic passages setting forth one's obligations towards parents, it is worthnoting that they, particularly the mother, are portrayed as one's benefactors. One is reminded of how they faced hardships in bringing one up. As thanksgiving one should be kind to them. This fits in with the larger scheme of things Islamic. For Allah is the benefactor *par excellence*. It is on account of Allah's favour that one is blessed with parents who selflessly and lovingly spend all that they have for their children. In comparison, Allah's concern and bounties for His servants are beyond measure. One should be thankful, in the first place, to Allah and then to one's parents. Islam infuses gratitude into the hearts of believers. Prompted by the same they profusely thank Allah. And on a much narrower scale, a Muslim is naturally drawn towards his parents out of gratitude for them.

Another striking point about the Qur'ānic directive is that one should treat one's parents well in their old age. This pointed reference to their old age rests on several important considerations. First, they need greater care and attention as they turn physically and emotionally infirm. At this juncture they are especially sensitive to any neglect shown them. Being physically weak, they are more prone to being irritable and unable to exercise self-restraint. At times, they may behave irrationally, placing such demands on their children which may be hard to meet. It is in the face of all these irritants that one is directed by the Qur'ān to treat them with love and respect. Man is reminded of his own infancy and childhood when he placed too many demands on his parents and they cheerfully bore all such hardships. In turn, one should bear with his parents' foibles and temperamental problems.

Against this backdrop, one realises the significance of the prayers taught by the Qur'ān to man, for seeking strength from Allah, which may enable one to treat one's parents well. Obviously, Allah's mercy can help one discharge this difficult duty. Furthermore, it explains why many *aḥādīth* highlight the importance of this obligation and speak of Allah's reward and punishment for one's treatment of one's parents. It is, no doubt, quite a task to maintain excellent relations with parents consistently. At the same time, it is vital for protecting and upholding the social fabric. Accordingly, many *aḥādīth* graphically spell out Allah's reward on this count. Take the following *aḥādīth* as illustrative.

- It is related on Ibn 'Abbās's authority that the Prophet made the following observation: A dutiful son who only looks at his parents with love and kindness will earn the reward due for *Ḥajj* for each glance of his. Someone asked: If one casts such a glance one hundred times a day, will he get the reward one hundred times? The Prophet replied: Yes, he will be credited with this reward for each glance. Almighty Allah's treasure is not diminished on account of even such generous and ample rewards. (Bayhaqī)

- Abū Bakrah reports that the Prophet said: While Allah may defer the punishment for one's sins until the Day of Recompense, one guilty of denying one's parents their due and disobeying them is punished in this world itself. This is in addition to the punishment to be inflicted in the Hereafter. (Bayhaqī)

The Qur'ānic passages urging the good treatment of parents make pointed reference to man's total submission to Allah in this world and his ultimate return to Him. The point pressed home is that one's excellent attitude towards one's parents should flow from one's wholesale surrender to Allah. As part of this and in accordance with divine command one should treat one's parents well. One should not be prompted by any material interest or selfish motive such as that of eliciting praise from others in serving one's parents. Rather, one's eyes should be set on the Hereafter, and, in view of divine reward, one should be kind to one's parents, as this will win Allah's pleasure in the Hereafter. In sum, a Muslim's conduct including his relationship with parents should be governed by Allah's commands recorded in the Qur'ān and elaborated in *Ḥadīth*.

Related Qur'ānic passages for self-study

- al-Baqarah 2:83
- al-Nisā' 4:36
- al-An'ām 6:151
- Ibrāhīm 14:41
- al-Isrā' 17:23-25
- al-Naml 27:149
- al-'Ankabūt 29:8
- Nūḥ 71:28

17

Treating Children

[Abraham said] Praise be to Allah Who has granted me, despite my old age, Ishmael and Isaac. Truly my Lord hears supplications. O Lord! Make me one who establishes regular prayers, and also from among my progeny. O our Lord! Accept my supplication.

(Ibrāhīm 14:39-40)

THE Prophet Abraham (peace and blessings be upon him) is seen in the above passage thanking Allah profusely for having blessed him with two sons – Ishmael and Isaac. In the Islamic scheme of things, children are Allah's precious gift to man. One should regard them as a blessing from Allah. Those not fortunate enough to have a child should invoke Allah for the bestowal of this bounty. An instructive example is afforded by the Prophet Zakariyā's supplication:

My Lord! Bestow on me from Your presence a good offspring. Surely You hear supplications.

(Āl 'Imrān 3:38)

O my Lord! ... Bestow on me from Your presence an heir, who will inherit me and inherit the children of Jacob. And make him one with whom You are pleased.

O Zakariyā! We give you the glad tidings of a son, and his name shall be John.

(Maryam 19:5-7)

Allah responded positively to his plea and granted him John, who too, was one of Allah's Messengers.

While it is natural for man to perpetuate his race, he should make a point of invoking Allah for blessing him with a believing, pious child. This point permeates the above-quoted supplications of the Prophets Abraham and Zakariyā (peace and blessings be upon them).

When Allah appointed the Prophet Abraham (pbuh) the leader of mankind as a reward for his devotion to Allah, his instinctive supplication was that members of his progeny be elevated to the same status in the future. This was a perfectly natural response on his part. For it is innate in human nature to acquire all that is best for one's children. Allah, however, told Abraham that only such of his children would enjoy the exalted status of mankind's leaders as were true believers. Needless to add, it is imperative to ensure the Islamic upbringing of one's children. The Prophets Abraham and Jacob (peace and blessings be upon them) are seen expressing the same concern on their deathbed, as they assembled and addressed their children thus:

Recall when his Lord said unto Abraham: "Submit". He said: "I submit to the Lord of the worlds."

And Abraham enjoined the same to his sons and so did Jacob, saying: "O my sons! Surely Allah has chosen faith for you. So die not except as Muslims. Were you witnesses when death presented itself to Jacob, and when he said to his sons: What will you worship after me? They said: We shall worship your God, the God of your fathers, Abraham, Ishmael and Isaac, the one and only God. To Him we submit (in Islam)."

(al-Baqarah 2:132-133)

Luqmān's advice to his son stands out as the Qur'ānic role model for parents instructing their children in the articles of faith and inculcating in their supple minds the basic truths related to faith and morality:

And recall when Luqmān told his son by way of instruction:
O my son! Do not join in worship others with Allah. For false worship is indeed the highest wrongdoing.

O my son! If there be but the weight of a mustard seed and it were hidden in a rock, or anywhere in the heavens or on earth, Allah will bring it forth. For Allah is the Subtle, the Aware.
O my son! Establish regular prayer, enjoin what is lawful and forbid what is wrong. And bear patiently whatever may befall you. For this is the firmness of purpose in the conduct of affairs.
And turn not your cheek from men, nor walk on earth, full of pride. For Allah does not love any arrogant boaster. And be modest in your pace and lower your voice ...
Do you not see that the ship sails into the sea by the favour of Allah that He might show you of His signs? Surely in it are signs for every persevering, grateful heart.

(Luqmān 31:13, 16-19 and 31)

A shining example of imbibing the message of truth is represented by the Prophet Ishmael (peace and blessings be upon him). Even at a very young age he demonstrated the utmost devotion to his Creator, Allah, and to his sincere father, Abraham. Here is the instructive account of the son, Ishmael and his father, Abraham, displaying their total surrender to Allah:

[Abraham petitioned] "O my Lord! Grant me a pious son." So We gave him the good news of a gentle boy.
And when the son reached the age of serious work with him, Abraham said: "O my son! I have seen in a dream that I am slaughtering you. So what do you think?" He replied: "O my father! Do what you are commanded. You will find me, if Allah wills so, one full of patience and constancy."

Then when the two submitted themselves, and Abraham had laid Ishmael on his forehead for sacrifice, We called out to him: "O Abraham! You have already fulfilled the vision." Thus do We reward those who do right. For this was obviously a trial. And We ransomed him with a mighty sacrifice.

(al-Ṣaffāt 37:100-107)

As opposed to Ishmael's exemplary conduct as the son who professed and practised faith as instructed by his father, there is the example of the Prophet Noah's son. He refused to listen to his father's message and advice and perished disgracefully:

And Noah's ark moved on with them amidst waves like mountains, and Noah called out to his son, and he was apart: "O my son! Embark with us and be not with the unbelievers."
He replied: "I will betake myself to some mountain. It will save me from water." Noah said: "There is no protector today from the command of Allah, except for one on whom He has mercy." And a wave came between Noah and his son and his son was drowned.

(Hūd 11:41-43)

The above incident illustrates well the point that one's family background is of no relevance in matters of faith. As the Prophet Noah's son refused to embrace faith, he was punished in the same manner as other unbelievers were. Since the Prophet Abraham's son, Ishmael stood to the test of faith, he was amply rewarded. One should therefore, supplicate for and bring up such children who imbibe the message of faith. This point comes out more sharply in the following submission of true believers, as recorded in the Qur'ān:

O our Lord! Grant us wives and children who will be the comfort of our eyes. And make us the leaders of the pious ones.

(al-Furqān 25:74)

As pointed out by Daryābādī, these supplications for the granting of children indicate

> that Islam, unlike Christianity, does not regard this world as inherently bad, and does not reject family ties as an impediment to the service of God. Celibacy, far from being a handmaid of believers, is rather an impediment in His way.[1]

The Islamic position on the desirability of having children and a family life, as set forth in the Qur'ān and *aḥādīth*, rectifies the erroneous notion that celibacy is the sure means for attaining purity and piety. Islam promoted the ideals of marriage and family life against the backdrop of society's wide acceptance of celibacy. The following historical account indicates how the fallacious notion of celibacy had crept into every religious tradition:

> Celibacy is the religiously motivated commitment to life-long abstention from sexual relations. Evidence of such commitments abounds in all major religions, e.g. Priests of Cybele, Buddhist monks, nuns, and Roman Catholic priests in the Christian tradition, and occasionally among Jewish sects ... In the Christian tradition ... celibacy is required of monks and nuns in religious orders as a sign of total commitment to Christ or, in the case of nuns, marriage to the Church.[2]

Another common fallacy corrected by Islam with regard to children relates to their sustenance. On being blessed with a child one should believe all the more that Allah is the sole Provider and Sustainer. For one affords to support one's child as Allah increases one's sustenance. The Qur'ānic assertion about Allah providing for everyone assumes greater meaning in the context of the ghastly practice of infanticide in pre-Islamic Arabia. Out of fear of poverty, parents used to bury their babies alive. Daryābādī makes the following apt observation on the Islamic stance on children:

> The practice of infanticide has been almost universal, neither Greece nor Rome being immune. So the reform effected by Islam was a world reform ... the reference may also be to the practice of *coitus interruptus* and other methods of birth control.[3]

The same fear of poverty lurks behind state-sponsored family planning drives in our own times. The Qur'ān strikes at the roots of this baseless apprehension, declaring:

Do not kill your children for fear of want. We shall provide for you and for them.

(al-An'ām 6:151)

Surely lost are they who slay their children foolishly and without knowledge. They have forbidden what Allah has provided for them; a fabrication against Allah. Surely they have gone astray and have not become the guided ones.

(al-An'ām 6:140)

Surely your Lord increases the provision for whom He will, and restricts it in a certain measure. For He knows and beholds all of His creatures.
Do not kill your children for fear of want. We provide for them and for you. Their killing is a great sin.

(al-Isrā' 17:30-31)

As we noted earlier, both the Prophets Abraham and Zakariyā (peace and blessings be upon them) were granted children in response to their fervent supplications for the same. Allah bestowed children on them, the Qur'ān states, from His presence. All this underscores the importance of children in the Islamic worldview.

Children being Allah's special gift are to be treated with great care. Regarding children, parents' first and foremost duty is to arrange for their instruction in the articles of Islamic faith and their moral training in line with the Islamic value system. This alone transforms children into being the coolness of parents' eyes in both worlds. That this is a parental responsibility is clearly spelled out in the following Qur'ānic passage which also carries a note of severe warning:

O Believers! Save yourselves and your families from the Fire, of which the fuel is men and stones.

(al-Taḥrīm 66:6)

When the above verse was revealed, 'Umar ibn al-Khaṭṭāb sought the Prophet's clarification on its import, submitting: "O Messenger of Allah! It is perfectly clear that one must save oneself against Hellfire by adhering to Allah's command and refraining from sin. But how can one guard one's wife, children and other family members against it?" To this the Prophet replied: "You should dissuade them from doing all that displeases Allah and exhort them to perform such deeds which may help them win Allah's pleasure. So doing, you can defend them against Hellfire."[4] The same point is reiterated in another *ḥadīth* thus: The Prophet said: "May Allah have mercy on him who instructs his wife and children that their prayers, fasting, paying *zakāh* and giving money to the poor and the orphan would facilitate their entry into Paradise. By the same token, one will be inflicted with severe punishment on the Day of Judgement, who fails to teach his wife and children the essential articles of faith."[5]

According to the Qur'ān, children are placed as a trust with their parents. In this sense, they constitute a test for the parents. For man is prone to crossing the limits prescribed by Allah in his love for his children. For example, he may resort to means of unlawful earning in order to meet the demands of his children. Likewise, it is a common sight that one's social relations within one's immediate family and with one's neighbours turn sour as one blindly takes sides with one's children in a quarrel, even though the latter may be guilty. Out of one's doting one is thus liable to neglect even one's religious duties. For these reasons the Qur'ān warns man:

> *And know that your wealth and your children are a temptation. With Allah is immense reward.*
>
> (al-Anfāl 8:27-28)

> *Your wealth and your children are a trial. Allah, with Him is mighty reward.*
>
> (al-Taghābun 64:15)

These Qur'ānic remarks are elucidated insightfully by Daryābādī thus:

> These [children and wealth] are a trial, a test, to find out who mishandles these gifts of God and who uses them in a proper and legitimate way. Note that temptation is not synonymous with sin. Nor is love of children or fondness for wealth, in itself, sinful. Such emotions, appetites, instincts, etc. are part of man, as it has pleased God to make him so. It is only human will that can shape them into sins.[6]

Children represent a trial constituted by Allah in the sense that one's commitment to faith is tested thus. Often does one's interests clash in so far as one's love for one's children might prompt one to do something that is forbidden by Allah. The Qur'ān therefore advises man that he should not be swerved so much by his love for his children which may ruin his prospects in the Next Life. Rather, one's loyalty and love should be exclusively for Allah.

Children constitute a trial, for any unlawful act done for their sake may incur Allah's punishment. They are the means for both earning reward and for incurring punishment. Significantly enough, the Qur'ānic passages about children also speak of Allah's great reward for those who pass this test.

The following incident involving the Prophet's Companion, Abū Lubābah illustrates how one's children pose a difficult test for man. At the end of the siege of Banū Qurayẓah, the Prophet proposed the name of Sa'd ibn Mu'ādh as the arbiter to decide the fate of Banū Qurayẓah who had violated the pact with the Muslims. Members of Banū Qurayẓah, however, insisted that this assignment be given to Abū Lubābah. Since Abū Lubābah was an *Anṣār* who had been Banū Qurayẓah's neighbour for years, they expected him to act leniently towards them. The Prophet agreed to this arrangement and Abū Lubābah was entrusted with the assignment. During negotiations, in a weak moment, however, he divulged the Prophet's strategy to Banū Qurayẓah. Soon he realised his mistake, which was rooted partly in his concern for the safety and security of his children who were surrounded by Banū Qurayẓah. This amounted to acting treacherously towards Allah and His Messenger. Ashamed of his misconduct, he could not muster the courage to face the Prophet.

So he went straight to the Prophet's mosque and tied himself to a pillar there, vowing that he would be in the same state till his repentance was accepted by Allah. For seven days he was in this state of self-imposed penance. When Allah informed the Prophet of His acceptance of Abū Lubābah's repentance, he secured his release.

To sum up, man should regard children as an invaluable favour from Allah, ensure their Islamic upbringing and not cross the *Sharī'ah* limits out of love for them. For one will be held accountable on the Day of Judgement as to how one treated one's children.

Related Qur'ānic passages for self-study

- al-Baqarah 2:128
- Maryam 19:42-50
- Saba' 34:37
- al-Munāfiqūn 63:9
- al-Taghābun 64:15

References

1. Daryābādī, *The Glorious Qur'ān*, op. cit., p. 656.
2. *Chambers Dictionary of Beliefs and Religions*, op. cit., p. 90.
3. Daryābādī, *The Glorious Qur'ān*, op. cit., p. 279.
4. *Rūḥ al-Ma'ānī*. See the commentary on 66:6.
5. Ibid.
6. Daryābādī, *The Glorious Qur'ān*, op. cit., p. 339.

Treating Husbands/Wives Well

And among Allah's signs in this is that He created for you mates from among yourselves, that you may dwell in peace with them. And He has put love and mercy between your hearts. Surely in that are signs for those who reflect.

(al-Rūm 30:21)

MARITAL bliss is accorded such importance in Islam that the Qur'ān speaks of gender relations as one of Allah's signs. Throughout the Qur'ān the unity of mankind is emphasised, with Allah being the sole Creator of both men and women.

O mankind! Fear Allah Who created you of a single soul, and He created from it its mate and out of the two He multiplied countless men and women.

(al-Nisā' 4:1)

The same origin of man and woman, as stated in the above passage signifies

the essential equality of men and women as human beings. It was not in Islam, but in Christianity, to its eternal shame, that

> woman was considered "an inferior, empty-headed moron; for several days in each month she was so unclean as to require secluding like a leper. The Council of Trent, in the sixteenth century, was dubious about her possessing a soul." (A. Forbath (Ed.), *Love, Marriage, Jealousy*, London, 1939, p. 371.) The Council, let it be further noted, was of the greatest significance in the history of the Roman Church.[1]

Apart from stressing the essential equality of men and women, the Qur'ān brands marriage as a social institution of the utmost importance. Allah's Messengers had wives and children, (al-Ra'd 13:38). The Qur'ān speaks particularly highly of Pharaoh's believing wife. The exemplary conduct of the Prophet Muḥammad's wives, especially of Khadījah and 'Ā'ishah in their efforts to spread Islam underscores their contribution to faith. In Islam, unlike Christianity, marriage is not an impediment to spiritual advancement:

> Marriage in the view of the apostle Paul (1 Corinthians 7), may sometimes be foregone in order to serve God, unfettered by the responsibilities of family life. This is the case with monasticism and the unmarried priesthood of the Roman Catholic Church, where it is compulsory not to marry.[2]

By contrast, Islam exhorts man to marry. The poor are assured of an increase in sustenance after marriage. This exhortation is directed at everyone. All members of the community should facilitate marriage, for this is the prerequisite for family life so strongly recommended by Islam:

> *Marry those among you who are single, or the virtuous ones among your male and female slaves. If they are poor, Allah will enrich them out of His bounty. Allah encompasses all and He knows all things.*
>
> (al-Nūr 24:32)

There are many reasons why Islam encourages marriage. Rather, in the Islamic scheme of things it occupies pride of place. Almost all Allah's messengers described in the Qur'ān had a family. This, thus, strikes a severe blow to the erroneous notions of piety and monasticism.

First, marriage is the means, as ordained by Allah, for the perpetuation of the human race. As part of this design Allah has imbued man with a strong sexual drive to reproduce and infused into him such overflowing love for his children that he bears all the difficulties in rearing them. It is not, therefore, surprising to note the following Qur'ānic directive, exhorting man to approach his wife so as to bless them both with children, if Allah so wills:

Your wives are a tillage for you. So approach your tilth when or how you will. And do some good act for your souls beforehand. And fear Allah. And know that you are to meet Him (in the Hereafter) and give these glad tidings to the believers.

(al-Baqarah 2:223)

The metaphor of "tilth" for wife is pregnant with overtones of the underlying objective behind marriage, namely, begetting and rearing children. According to the distinguished Arabic lexicographer, E.W. Lane, "tillage signifies the soil which receives the seeds and grows the plant. The import of the verse is: your wives are unto you things wherein you sow offspring; they are thus likened to places that are ploughed for sowing".

Moreover, the pointed reference to fear of Allah and to meeting Allah in the Hereafter underscores the seriousness and importance of the husband-wife relationship. Those guilty of destroying marital relations should fear Allah and consider its terrible consequences in the Hereafter.

Much more evocative and suggestive is the other Qur'ānic metaphor for describing the husband-wife relationship:

Permitted to you, on the night of fasts, is the approach to your wives. They are your garments and you are their garments.

(al-Baqarah 2:187)

Daryābādī interprets the metaphor of "garment" in terms of the constant inseparable companionship between husband and wife:

> [It is] expressive of close intimacy, identity of interest, mutual comfort and confidence, the mutual upholding of each other's reputation and credit, the mutual respect for each other's secrets, mutual affection, and mutual consolation in misfortune. The whole character of the one becomes an open book to the other. The wedded pair cease to belong to themselves; they now belong to each other, sharing each other's joys, sorrows glories and shame.[3]

Islam views marriage as a formidable bond, to be executed sincerely and seriously. It prescribes marriage as a perfectly acceptable and desirable social institution which should slam the door on any sexual relationship outside marriage. Furthermore, marriage partners should keep in mind all along the sanctity of their relationship. It should not be degraded for only gratifying lust and unbridled sexual urges:

> *Allowed to you are chaste believing women and chaste women of those given the Book before you, when you have given them their dower taking them in wedlock, desiring chastity, not lewdness, nor taking them as secret mistresses.*
>
> (al-Mā'idah 5:5)

The repeated reference to chastity in the context of marriage brings into sharper light the solemn and sacred nature of marriage. Chastity is an important criterion for marriage in Islam, as is also evident from this Qur'ānic enactment, permitting marriage with handmaids for those who cannot afford to marry free women:

> *And he among you who does not have the means to wed free believing women, he may wed such of the believing handmaids whom your right hands possess. And Allah knows well your belief. You are one from another: wed them with the consent of their owners, and give*

them their dower, according to what is reasonable. They should be chaste, not lustful, not taking secret lovers.

(al-Nisā' 4:25)

Apart from ensuring chastity and sexual fidelity, another great advantage of marriage, according to the Qur'ān, is that it provides the marriage partners with mutual love, peace and joy which are vital for man's mental, emotional and social equilibrium. It helps one lead a balanced, well-poised life. Thus marital bliss is portrayed graphically in the Qur'ān:

Allah created you from a single soul and He created of him his mate in order that he might find comfort in her and live with her in love. When they are united, she bears a light burden and carries it about. When she grows heavy, they both pray to Allah, their Lord: If You grant us a goodly child, we shall ever be grateful.

(al-A'rāf 7:189)

As elaborated by Daryābādī, the above passage implies various facets to the marriage relationship: "... of love in youth, of companionship in middle age, and of care and attendance in old age".[4] Equally striking is their shared parenting, fervent desire for and sincere commitment to get and bring up children. The overarching goal of their tie, nonetheless, should be to earn Allah's pleasure, as is clear from their supplication, reflective of their thankfulness to Him. On another occasion, marital bliss is projected as one of the wonderful signs of Allah's creative power. Undoubtedly, without this special arrangement devised by Allah, the married couple, strangers to each other before entering their matrimonial alliance, could not develop such a deep, intimate relationship:

Among Allah's signs is that He created for you mates from among yourselves, that you may find repose in them; He has put love and mercy between you. Certainly in that are signs for those who reflect.

(al-Rūm 30:21)

Once again, the Qur'ān draws attention to the features of mutual love and companionship in marriage. Husband and wife are a source of invaluable solace to each other; marriage in Islam is thus the soothing element of life. Quite opposed to this is the Church's stance on the issue:

> We cannot but notice, even in the greatest of the Christian fathers, a lamentably low estimation of women, and consequently of the marriage relationship. Even St. Augustine can see no justification for marriage, except in a grave desire deliberately adopted of having children, and in accordance with this view, all married intercourse, except for this single purpose, is honestly condemned. This idea of the mutual society, help and comfort that the one ought to have of the other, both in prosperity and adversity, hardly existed, and hardly yet exists.[5]

It is in recognition of the pivotal and influential role of marriage in man's life that Islam insists that a Muslim should take only a believing woman as his marriage partner. Islam admits no compromise in matters of faith. Since the highly intimate relationship of marriage might pose a danger to faith, particularly of the children, Islam asks Muslims:

> *Do not marry unbelieving women (idolaters) until they believe. A believing slave girl is better than an unbelieving woman, although the latter pleases you. And do not marry (your girls) to unbelievers until they believe. A believing slave is better than an unbeliever, though the latter pleases you. The unbelievers call you to the Hellfire, while Allah calls you to Paradise and to forgiveness by His Grace. He makes His signs clear to mankind that they may celebrate His praise.*
>
> (al-Baqarah 2:221)

It is worth clarifying that the Bible too, prohibits marriage between Israelites and non-Israelites, as is decreed in the Old Testament, the Talmud and the Rabbinical codes. Illustrative of this is the following Biblical passage which reverberates the Qur'ānic stance on this issue:

"Be you not yoked together with unbelievers. For what fellowship has righteousness with unright-eousness? And what in common has light with darkness?" (2 Corinthians 6:14)

Allah being man's Creator knows human nature, its strengths and weaknesses well. Accordingly, Islam has made allowance for polygamy and divorce as well. Orientalists and those given to Islam-bashing have greatly maligned the Islamic provision for polygamy. While making a show of their pious horror they dub it as something monstrous, immoral and unfair to women. So doing, they turn a blind eye to history, the male mindset and to socio-economic realities. It should be stated at the outset that since the beginning of history, polygamy has been practised in all civilisations and religions. The Prophets Abraham, Jacob, Moses, David and Solomon (peace and blessings be upon them) each had more than one wife. Given this, there is nothing outrageous about this Qur'ānic provision. Rather, the Qur'ān restricted the number of wives to only four and, more importantly, it alerted man to the demands of justice and fairness in practising polygamy. The concept of justice is to the fore in the Qur'ānic passages on this provision:

Marry women of your choice, two or three or four, but if you; fear that you shall not be able to deal justly with them, then only one …

(al-Nisā' 4:3)

And you are not able to be fair and just between wives, even though you may like to do so. But do not turn away from one woman altogether, so as to leave her suspended. If you come to a friendly understanding and practise self-restraint, Allah is Ever-Forgiving, Most Merciful.

(al-Nisā' 4:129)

As to the practice of polygamy, it was the rule among the Eastern people before the Prophet Muhammad's time. When we see thousands of miserable women who crowd the streets of Western towns during the night, we must surely feel that it does not lie in Western mouths to reproach Islam for its polygamy. It is better for a woman, happier for a woman, more respectable for a woman, to live in Mohammadan polygamy, united to one man only, with the legitimate child in her arms surrounded with respect than to be seduced, cast out in the streets – perhaps with an illegitimate child outside the pale of the law – unsheltered and uncared for to become a victim of any passer by, night after night rendered incapable of motherhood, despised of all.[6]

Islam being the natural way has spelled out clearly the respective roles and responsibilities of husband and wife. This division of labour, does not imply one's superiority and the other's inferiority. Rather, it recognises the two as equal partners, each one discharging his/her set of duties for a happy, peaceful family life, which, in turn, augurs well for children in particular, and society in general. The husband's role, broadly speaking, embraces economic pursuits. For he is better fitted as the breadwinner. The husband also enjoys the right to divorce, though the wife too, may secure a separation. While granting the husband the authority to divorce, the Qur'ān makes it plain that women have the same rights which men have. Husband and wife complement each other. The relationship between them is one characterised by interdependence:

Divorced women shall wait concerning themselves for three monthly periods ... And their husbands have the better right to take them back in that period, if they wish for reconciliation. And women have rights similar to the rights against them, according to what is honourable. And for men there is a degree above them.

(al-Baqarah 2:228)

Daryābādī elucidates the thrust of the above passage thus:

Women have rights quite similar to those of men. This bold and explicit declaration of the rights of women centuries and centuries before Mill dreamt of writing on *The Subjection of Women* has no parallel in the pages of other Divine Scriptures. Contrast this with the attitude of the Bible which as a punishment for Eve makes the wife a subject of her husband who is to rule over her. According to the Old Testament, woman is responsible for the fall of man, and this became the cornerstone of Christian teaching.[7]

Alongside equality of rights, the Qur'ān states the excellence man has over woman by dint of his constitution and instructs the wife to obey him so as to ensure a happy, married life:

Men are protectors and maintainers of women because Allah has given the one more strength than the other, and because men support women by their means. Therefore, righteous women are devoutly obedient, and guard in the husband's absence by the aid and protection of Allah.

(al-Nisā' 4:34)

At the same time men are instructed to

Live with them [wives] honourably. If you dislike them, it may be that you dislike a thing, and Allah brings about through it a great deal of good.

(al-Nisā' 4:19)

The following directive is in the same vein:

Seek women in marriage with gifts from your property, desiring chastity not lust, seeking that you derive benefit from them.

(al-Nisā' 4:24)

And when you have divorced your women and they fulfil the term of their waiting period, then either retain them honourably or release them kindly; and do not retain them to hurt so that you may cross the limits. And whoever does so wrongs his own soul. And do not hold Allah's commandments in mockery.

(al-Baqarah 2:231)

The Qur'ānic message is loud and clear: men enjoying authority are exhorted to be fair and lenient towards their wives. They should love and respect their wives and bear with the latter's weaknesses. In extreme cases, they may divorce their wives as a last resort. Nonetheless, wives are not to be harmed or exploited. Allah's commands are specific and hence these must be followed seriously. Furthermore, the institution of marriage lies at the core of society. It should not be weakened in any case. In Islam the wife is not some commodity owned by her husband. She has her own set of obligations and rights which must be granted to her.

The Qur'ān instructs the wife too, to embody such virtues and values which are central to a happy marriage. Mention is made, in particular, of sexual fidelity and having an understanding of the husband whereby his preferences are accommodated:

> *Righteous women are devout and obedient and guard themselves in the husband's absence by the aid and protection of Allah.*
> *As to those women on whose part you fear disloyalty and ill-conduct, admonish them (first), next refuse to share their beds, and last beat them. But if they obey you, do not seek a way against them.*
>
> (al-Nisā' 4:34)

> *O wives of the Prophet! You are not like any other women, if you fear Allah. Be not soft in speech, lest one in whose heart is a disease should be moved with desire. But speak honourably.*
> *And stay in your houses, and do not display yourselves, as did the pagans of the* Jāhilīyah *period. And establish Prayer, and give* Zakāh *and obey Allah and His Messenger.*
>
> (al-Aḥzāb 33:32-33)

> *And say to the believing women that they should lower their gaze and guard their modesty. They should not display their beauty and adornment except what appears of it. They should draw scarves over their bosoms.*
>
> (al-Nūr 24:31)

To recapitulate, the Qur'ān brings home the following points about the husband-wife relationship.

- Marriage is both a vital and sacred institution, part of the divine plan for the propagation of the human race and for man's and woman's biological needs.
- Husband and wife should be a source of mutual solace and strength for each other, a point borne out by the Qur'ānic metaphors for the husband-wife relationship.
- Since this relationship is very intimate, the Qur'ān forbids marriage with a polytheistic man or woman. In the face of such differences on faith, there cannot be any understanding and sincerity.
- Both husband and wife should bear in mind all along their fear of Allah and their accountability on the Day of Judgement when discharging their obligations to each other, and in their general treatment of their spouse.
- The Qur'ān cites the role model of the pious wife of Pharaoh, characterised by her enviable commitment to faith. This may be supplemented with the excellent examples of the Prophet Muḥammad's wives, namely Khadījah and 'Ā'ishah. The Prophet's own life stands out as a model of a caring and loving husband. Following in their footsteps we can perform well as husband and wife.

Related Qur'ānic passages for self-study

- al-Baqarah 2:236
- al-Nisā' 4:128
- al-Nūr 24:30-33
- al-Ṭalāq 65:7

References

1. Daryābādī, *The Glorious Qur'ān*, op. cit., p. 156.
2. *Chambers Dictionary of Beliefs and Religions*, op. cit., p. 325.
3. Daryābādī, *The Glorious Qur'ān*, op. cit., p. 65.
4. Ibid., p. 330.
5. *Dictionary of Christian Antiquities*, edited by Smith and Cheetham, London, 1900, vol. 2, p. 1909.
6. Annie Besant, as quoted by Daryābādī, *The Glorious Qur'ān*, p. 157
7. Ibid., p. 85.

19

Good Social Behaviour

The believers are brothers in faith. So make peace and reconciliation between your brethren. And fear Allah so that you may receive His mercy.

O Believers! Let not some men among you laugh at others. It may be that the latter are better than the former. Let not some women laugh at others. It may be that the latter are better than the former. And do not criticise one another, nor call them by offensive nicknames. It is bad to commit sin after professing belief. And those who do not repent are wrongdoers.

O Believers! Avoid suspicion as much as possible. For in some cases suspicion is a sin. And do not spy on and backbite one another. Would any of you like to eat the flesh of your dead brother? You would abhor it. And fear Allah. Allah accepts repentance and is Most Merciful.

O mankind! We have created you from a single pair of a male and female. And We have made you into nations and tribes so that you may know one another. The most honoured of you in the sight of Allah is he who is the most pious of you. And Allah has full knowledge and is well acquainted with all things.

(al-Ḥujūrat 49:10-13)

AVOIDING any harm to fellow human beings is the main concern of this code of conduct for social life. The passage opens on a note of human fraternity and unity. Equally significant is the point that the passage concludes with the same message of mankind's unity. While discarding all notions of kinship based on ethnicity, language, colour or caste, the Qur'ān asserts the bond of faith as the unifying force. All Muslims are brothers of one another on account of sharing the same set of beliefs, though they may differ greatly from one another in outward features. This characteristic of Islam prompts an Orientalist to concede the point:

> A Muslim is Muslim first and a Turk, an Afghan, or an Arab afterwards, and this is no mere formula or figure of speech. Instead the vast assemblage of peoples and of tongues to whom the Prophet of Arabia, by teaching them to worship the one true God, has given a bond of union stronger than any tie of blood or nation.[1]

History bears testimony to the fact that Muslims as a community have demonstrated numerous instances of solidarity, cutting across barriers of race, colour or language. In so doing, Muslims act on the following *aḥādīth* regarding the bond of unity to be found in Islam: The Prophet said: "None of you has faith until he desires for his brother what he desires for himself." In the same vein is his other observation: "To abuse a Muslim is an evil deed, and to fight him, an act of unbelief." (Bukhārī) That Islam inculcated this ideal of the equality and unity of all Muslims among its immediate addressees – the Arabs – is all the more striking in view of the fact that the Arabs of the day were very particular about their clan identity, tribal pride and ancestral fame. The ideal of social equality, as professed and practised by early Muslims, was the key to the phenomenal spread of Islam across all parts of the world. The exploited and the deprived reeling under yokes of bondage saw Islam with its teachings and practice of equality and fraternity as their champion and warmly embraced it in large numbers.

On the import of the opening verse of the passage M. Manazir Ahsan makes this perceptive comment:

> The basic idea which Islam wants to bring home is the equality of mankind and the establishment of all relationships on the basis of faith ... a relationship which stands above that of blood. If a blood relationship stands in the way of Islam, it is to be rejected in favour of faith.[2]

The Qur'ān does not turn a blind eye to the human weakness of quarrel, dispute and even war. Accordingly, it exhorts Muslims to make peace among hostile individuals or groups. Of special note in this context is the Qur'ānic use of the expressions "brothers in faith" and "fear of Allah". Even while mutual relations among some Muslims are strained, they should not forget that they are essentially brothers of one another. They should sort out their differences in a brotherly manner, characterised by affection, love and sincerity. Moreover, they should realise all along that Allah, their supreme Lord, constantly watches them. Any injustice done by either party cannot escape His notice. It will, however, provoke His anger and punishment which will destroy them wholly. They should therefore desist from doing any wrong to fellow Muslims and behave only in such a way as may earn them His mercy. The main idea of Muslim brotherhood adumbrated in the verse is elucidated in several *aḥādīth*, of which the following are cited as instances in point:

> Believers are to one another like the bricks in a building, in which every brick is supported and strengthened by another.
>
> (Bukhārī)

> Believers represent a single body in terms of their mutual love, kindness and affection. If one part of the body is hurt, the entire body feels its pain.
>
> (Bukhārī and Muslim)

> The life, property and honour of one Muslim is sacred for other Muslims.
>
> (Muslim)

Allah being man's Creator knows best what might damage cordial social relations, as a result of weaknesses in human nature. The passage under study goes to great lengths in identifying and remedying these human failings. Mention is made first of the fairly common tendency of laughing at others. Both men and women are equally prone to doing this. Strikingly enough, the Qur'ān addresses both men and women separately, asking them to desist from it. For the men or women so ridiculed may be better than those scoffing at them. What actually accounts for issuing this directive separately to men and women is that Islam does not envisage any intermixing of men and women. It does not, therefore, admit the possibility that men may mock women and *vice versa*. For they should not and cannot gain such acquaintance with the opposite sex, as may result in taking them as the butt of ridicule and mockery. Repetition of the directive is also aimed at emphasising the evil of such a practice. Laughing at others may take many different forms, as is pointed out thus:

> … copying someone's voice, laughing at his words, face or dress, and making gestures so as to attract attention to others' weaknesses. The underlying idea behind this act is to express one's superiority by undermining the prestige of others. This is regarded as character-assassination in Islam, and is abhorred in the same way as physical attack and persecution.[3]

Since mocking others amounts to attacking their honour and prestige, it is bound to strain social relations. The victim too might even resort to revenge. As a result, the social fabric is damaged, giving rise to many more evils. Islam therefore, strikes at the root of this common human failing of laughing at someone else's expense.

Another habit that deals a severe blow to mutual love and understanding is the tendency to criticise and blame others for offences, both real and imaginary. Needless to add, acrimonious remarks made against others are always counter-productive. The blame game is endless, with each party projecting the other in the worst possible light. Far from promoting the Islamic value system, this tendency creates fissures and ruptures in community life. Such actions and reactions run counter to the Islamic ideal of Muslim brotherhood. At another place too, the Qur'ān condemns the practice of slandering:

> *Woe to every kind of scandalmonger and backbiter, who piles up wealth and lays it by, thinking that his wealth will make him last forever. By no means! He will surely be thrown into that which breaks to pieces. And what would explain to you that which breaks to pieces? It is the fire of Allah kindled to a blaze.*
>
> (al-Humazah 104:1-6)

Using offensive nicknames is a variation of slander. The Qur'ān makes a point of prohibiting this as well. For, like mocking and slandering others, it disrupts cordial social relations. The victim may avenge himself or he may harbour ill-feelings against those who show disrespect towards him. In either case, social relations are bound to be affected. The Qur'ān is so particular about maintaining and promoting social harmony that it mentions, one by one, these irritants and urges man to shun them. For curbing these the Qur'ān goes a step further in asking man to be conscious all along of the All-Hearing, All-Seeing Allah and of the terrible consequences of such misdeeds in the Hereafter.

At the close of the verse these misdeeds, which harm fellow human beings, are branded as acts of wickedness. Muslims are reminded that after having professed belief, they should have nothing to do with any wicked act. As for those who refuse to pay any heed to these warnings and persist in such misdeeds, they are dubbed as wicked. The note of warning is clear and emphatic. Little wonder then that one comes across several reports about the Prophet's Companions that they made a point of shunning such behaviour. 'Abdullāh ibn Mas'ūd is on record as exclaiming: "I dread laughing at even a dog, lest I be turned into a dog." (Qurṭubī)

Verse 12 marks the extension of the same moral code. The focus shifts to those weaknesses which generally creep into a community as a whole and its behavioural pattern. Once again, the objective is to promote good social behaviour among members of the community and also towards others who are not part of the faith community. The directive starts by striking a blow at the root cause of all quarrels and conflicts – suspecting others and ascribing bad motives to all of their actions. If one does not check this tendency, it might make one's own life miserable. While one should be on one's guard regarding one's interests and not act in a gullible way, one should not take everyone as an enemy. Suspicion breeds hostility which eventually results in severing ties and relationships. The Qur'ān dubs such suspicion as a sin for it prompts one to doubt someone else's integrity and to interpret an action in the worst possible terms.

Closely related to suspicion is the human weakness of spying on others in order to find out their secrets. Also included under this heading are the following: "Bugging, reading someone's letters, peeping into someone's house, investigating someone's financial, private and family affairs."[4]

Not only does Islam proclaim the sanctity of human life, property and honour, it also expects every member of the community to uphold the same. Accordingly, it forbids any interest in others' personal and private lives. The Prophet brought home the above point thus:

> Do not speak ill of fellow Muslims. Do not look for their failings and weaknesses. For one who looks for their weaknesses, his failings are identified by Allah. Such a person is destined to be disgraced.
>
> (Qurṭubī)

The Islamic norm that one's personal life should not be probed unnecessarily is illustrated best by the following incident in the early history of Islam, involving a person of such exalted stature as the Caliph 'Umar. Once on his nightly inspection round the Caliph 'Umar passed by a house, resounding with song and music. He jumped over the wall and found inside the house a man in a drunken state in the company of a woman who was playing music. Enraged, the Caliph asked the man to explain his misconduct. However, the man retorted thus: "O Caliph, if I have committed one sin, you stand guilty of three. Allah has forbidden us to spy on someone. Yet you did the same. He has commanded that one should enter a house after securing permission. You have violated this. Moreover, you have invaded my privacy." The Caliph realised that in his zeal to check evil he had not followed the social norms spelled out in the Qur'ān. He, therefore, did not press charges against the person. However, he instructed the latter to lead his life in accordance with Islamic morals and manners. The latter assured him that he would mend his ways.

Of all the social evils covered in the passage, backbiting is condemned in the strongest terms in view of its devastating impact on social relations. Backbiting is, however, a common practice, for it is an essential part of social talk and the main ingredient of gossip. Some indulge in it without even realising that they are doing wrong. As regards its definition and nature, the Prophet's observation is very instructive: He explains: "Saying something about your brother which he would dislike." Someone present in his company queried: "Does this amount to backbiting about someone, if what is said about him is true?" To this the Prophet replied: "If you say something untrue about him, it constitutes a false accusation", which is an equally heinous practice. It is worth clarifying that backbiting is forbidden, even if it is directed against non-Muslims.

So as to provoke revulsion towards backbiting the Qur'ān employs a graphic simile – eating the flesh of one's dead brother. On this Manazir Ahsan offers the following insightful interpretation:

> The idea underlying the simile is that by backbiting a brother consumes the honour of another brother who is not present on the occasion to protest or defend himself. Therefore it is expected of a Muslim that he should abhor *ghībah* (backbiting) in the same way as he shudders at the thought of eating carrion.[5]

The horrible punishment for it, as described by the Prophet, underscores the enormity of the crime:

> While relating his night journey and ascent to the heavens, the Prophet said: "I passed by some people who had nails of copper and were engaged constantly in scratching their faces and breast. When I enquired of Gabriel about them, I was told

that they were being punished thus for their backbiting and attacking others' honour.

(Abu Dāwūd.)

The verse condemning backbiting concludes, significantly enough, with reference to fear of Allah. For this serves as a highly effective deterrent against any inclination towards sin. Furthermore, attention is drawn to Allah's attributes of forgiveness and mercy. Those guilty of backbiting should sincerely repent and turn to Allah to receive the blessings of His boundless mercy.

These directives, asking man to refrain from social evil, are followed by certain truths, which further reinforce the above moral code. The concluding verse addresses the whole of mankind, as opposed to the preceding verses which are specific to believers. While shunning these abominable practices which destroy the social fabric, man should bear in mind the constant fundamental truth that Allah alone is the Creator and Lord. Therefore, all of His commands must be faithfully and sincerely followed. Moreover it is also worth remembering that all men and women, irrespective of colour, caste or creed are the children of the first pair of human beings on earth – Adam and Eve. Being Adam's children all men and women are alike and equal. They should not do anything which hurts others in any degree. The Qur'ān thus proclaims the specific unity of mankind with reference to a single, common progenitor. More remarkably, the verse demolishes all notions of gender, tribal, caste or ethnic superiority or inferiority in asserting that these are mere labels for easy identification. Being a member of a particular nation or tribe does not confer any honour or stigma on anyone. What really distinguishes one person from another is the degree of his or her faith and piety. Allah does not attach any importance to one's ethnic origin or any such label. He rewards and punishes man only in proportion to his or her faith and piety. Daryābādī's comment is quite illuminating in this respect:

> So the doctrine of a biologically chosen people, as a race apart, designed by nature to rule the world is not only positively

mischievous but also mythical. And this puts an end to the pseudo-science of racial biology, seeking to justify political ambitions, economic ends and class prejudice.[6]

This declaration of the unity and equality of mankind is interlinked with the above cited prohibition against mocking, reproaching and nicknaming others and of suspicion, slander and backbiting. For one indulges in the above out of one's own false pride and sense of superiority. The Qur'ān therefore, stresses the truth that all men and women are equal. Piety alone makes one superior to others. Given this, one should refrain all the more from hurting and harming others. The same note of social justice, and human equality and fraternity is to the fore in the Prophet's sermon at his farewell pilgrimage when he addressed a huge congregation of Muslims at 'Arafāt:

> No Arab is superior to a non-Arab and no non-Arab has any superiority over an Arab. No black has any superiority over a white person and no white over a black one. Piety alone confers superiority on one. All men are from Adam and Adam was made of clay.[7]

In the Qur'ānic passage under study the emphasis is on building cordial, happy social relations among men and women, regardless of their affiliations. The directives aim at forging and sustaining a mutually helpful and trustworthy community life, ensuring peaceful coexistence among all members of society. Social justice is the distinct message of the passage. It seeks to infuse such virtues which guarantee a happy, peaceful life for everyone. It resounds with a strong plea for a tension-free society, without social, emotional and psychological strains. The lesson of tolerance, forgiveness and cordial social relations is unmissable. If these directives are followed sincerely, we may construct a happy and peaceful society, free from public disorder and the resultant tendencies of violence and revenge.

Related Qur'ānic passages for self-study

- al-Nisā' 4:1
- al-An'ām 6:98
- al-A'rāf 7:189
- al-Furqān 25:54
- al-Zumar 39:6

References

1. Bosworth, *Mohammed and Mohammedanism*, London, 1874, p. 306.
2. M. Manazir Ahsan, *The Islamic Attitude to Social Relations in the light of Sūrah al-Ḥujurāt: Verses 10-12*, Leicester, Islamic Foundation, 1989, pp.8-9.
3. Ibid., p. 12.
4. Ibid., p. 17.
5. Ibid., p. 19.
6. Daryābādī, *The Glorious Qur'ān*, op. cit., p. 930.
7. A.R. Kidwai, "The Prophet's Sermon: Charter for Peace and Social Justice", *Ahlan wa Sahlan*, January 2004, p. 8.

20

Making Supplications to Allah

Our Lord! Give us good in the world and good in the Hereafter, and save us from the torment of the Hellfire.

(al-Baqarah 2:201)

THIS and many other supplications appear in the Qur'ān with a view to instructing man how to make supplications to Allah. In the Islamic scheme of things, supplications occupy pride of place. Man being Allah's servant and fully dependent on Him should turn to Him for everything and by the same token express thanks for all that he has. This is an integral part of devotional worship in Islam. Significantly enough, the opening *sūrah* of the Qur'ān, al-Fātiḥah, which every Muslim is obliged to recite in every prayer, represents the spirit and tenor of supplication. Take the following verses of the *sūrah* as illustrative.

Guide us to the straight way, the way of those whom You have favoured, not the way of those who have incurred Your wrath, nor of those who have gone astray.

(al-Fātiḥah 1:6-7)

As the Prophet succinctly put it: "A supplication encapsulates the essence of worship." For it marks a direct communion between Allah and His servant. A striking feature of supplication in Islam is that it does not involve any intermediary. In other major faiths, it is performed through the agency of clergy and priests. Islam, however, instructs that man should invoke Allah directly. Moreover, it is an emotionally and spiritually fulfilling exercise. Even when one's supplication is not granted, the act itself brings immense comfort and solace. For it provides one with an opportunity to turn wholly and humbly to one's Lord. One invokes Allah from the depths of one's heart and in a spirit of total self-surrender to Him.

Included in the Qur'ān and *Ḥadīth* collections are supplications for every occasion, encompassing all aspects of the human condition. On studying these one learns how to make supplications to Allah and also many features of the Islamic worldview, especially the relationship obtaining between Allah and man.

The supplication quoted above is amazingly comprehensive in its range. Having recited it, one need not ask Allah for anything else. The first striking point about this Qur'ānic supplication is the use of the plural "we/us". As a member of the broader universal community of believers, a Muslim asks Allah to do good not only to him but also for the whole community. This thus underscores the strong bond of fraternity and universality in Islam. The entreaty for being blessed with good in this world does not imply any craving for worldly, material goods. Rather, one seeks such divine blessing so as to fill one's life with good. Reference is also made to professing and practising such faith as is approved by Allah. Also included in this are the virtues of contentment, a readiness to live in the condition ordained by Allah, a fervour to persuade everyone to abide by Allah's guidance and the ability and strength to adhere to His way. As Islam does not recommend monasticism, one may petition Allah to meet one's basic needs. More important nonetheless, is salvation in the Hereafter and protection against Hellfire. Accordingly, a pointed reference is made to the same. This supplication thus caters for both worlds. Daryābādī offers the following perceptive interpretation of this supplication:

Note that the object desired and sought in prayer is not the world at all, but good, and good only in whatsoever it may be found – whether in this world or the Next. Contrast this with the Christian concept embodied in the reported saying of Christ: "My kingdom is not of this world." (John 18:36)[1]

Making supplications serves as a constant reminder of man's servitude to Allah, his total dependence on Him for everything – major or minor. Man becomes all the more aware of his inadequacies and failings, which spurs him to strive harder for his moral and spiritual development. Man's reliance on Allah in every respect of life and his utter helplessness are to the fore in this supplication:

Our Lord! Do not take us to task, if we forget or err. Do not place on us such burden which You did on those before us. Our Lord! Do not impose on us that for which we do not have strength. And pardon us, forgive us, and have mercy on us. You are our Lord, so make us triumph over the unbelievers.

(al-Baqarah 2:286)

Man is liable to err and forget divine guidance. What is, however, more important is that he should be conscious of this weakness and repent as soon as he realises the lapse committed by him. Islam does not presuppose man as an infallible creature, who does not do any wrong. For the Qur'ān even records the lapses of Allah's messengers. However, they soon repented and sought Allah's forgiveness. The above supplication thus teaches man this fundamental truth about sin and divine forgiveness. One should petition Allah for not putting him to the test. For it might be too hard for one to overcome temptation or suffering. Remarkably, the supplication deals with all three stages of salvation – i) the pardoning of sins by dint of not punishing someone, ii) forgiveness which might facilitate one's entry into Paradise, and iii) pouring mercy over one which represents final success in the Hereafter.

Another Qur'ānic supplication, made by the Prophet Abraham (peace and blessings be upon him), is worth remembering at all times. For it reminds us of our basic religious duty and of our ultimate end:

O my Lord! Make me one who establishes regular Prayer, and also raise such among my children, O our Lord. And accept my supplication.
O our Lord! Cover us with Your forgiveness – me, my parents and all the believers on the Day of Reckoning.

(Ibrāhīm 14:40-41)

Prayer is the cornerstone of Islamic faith and hence the emphasis on it in the above supplication. Sincerity consists in desiring for others the same as what one likes best for oneself. Accordingly, the supplication extends to children as well, that they too, should be particular and regular in offering prayer. It is Allah Who enables one to perform this important religious duty on which depends one's success in both worlds. Therefore, Allah's acceptance of this supplication is especially invoked. Equally important it is to attain His forgiveness and mercy which may offset one's lapses. The universality of Islam is evident from this supplication. For divine forgiveness is sought for parents and all Muslims. This alone will secure salvation on the Day of Judgement. Concern for the Hereafter should be constantly present in one's heart and mind. For it helps one follow the straight way steadily and so shun sin.

On assuming the office of Prophethood, Allah taught the Prophet Moses the following supplication which is full of meaning and instruction for every Muslim:

O my Lord! Expand for me my breast. Make my task easy for me. And remove the impediment from my speech, that they may understand my speech.

(Ṭā Hā 20:25-28)

This spells out some of the qualities and skills which are immensely helpful for a Muslim in sincerely professing faith and for preaching faith among others. The first and foremost is conviction, unassailable faith which is never shaken, no matter what trials and sufferings one may face. This conviction, which represents Allah's special favour, is a Muslim's bulwark against all the attacks on his faith, from both within and without. Apart from the Prophet Moses (peace and blessings be upon him), the Prophet Muḥammad (peace and blessings be upon him) too, was blessed with this at the beginning of his prophetic career, as is detailed in *Sūrah* al-Sharḥ. Every Muslim should strive to gain conviction in matters of faith and fervently pray to Allah to bestow the same upon him. One cannot accomplish anything, however minor, without Allah's help and support. A Muslim should therefore, invoke His patronage in all his affairs, as this will facilitate matters for him. Equally important is the skill of articulating one's views. For persuading others to embrace and act on the dictates of faith a Muslim should be equipped with persuasive speech. One should therefore, seek Allah's aid on this count. This plea for achieving the above qualities and skills may be appreciated better if one studies it in conjunction with the following supplication which was taught in particular to the Prophet Muḥammad (peace and blessings be upon him) and which he frequently recited: "O my Lord! Give me increase in knowledge," (Ṭā Hā 20:114). It is, nonetheless, worth clarifying that the reference is only to such knowledge which draws one closer to Allah: knowledge in its absolute, unbridled form, as witnessed today, is not intended. Islam urges man to attain only useful knowledge which may make him a better human being, and a better devotee of Allah. Knowledge which promotes godlessness, promiscuity and gross materialism is branded as ignorance in Islam.

Love for children is innate in human nature. Islam upholds the same in recounting the plea of some of Allah's Messengers, supplicating to Him that they be granted children. An instance in point is the Prophet Zakariyā's petition for a child, (al-Anbiyā' 21:89). More important, however, is the upbringing of children along Islamic lines and their unwavering commitment to faith. It is not therefore, surprising that the following supplication stresses these points:

> *O our Lord! Bestow on us the coolness of eyes from our wives and our children and make us the leader of the pious ones.*
>
> (al-Furqān 25:74)

The metaphor of cool eyes signifies that one feels gratified about someone's pious conduct. Allah's help is therefore invoked for making wives and children the source of our joy in terms of their devotion to faith and their pious behaviour. In other words, the plea is that they attain such heights of piety that they be the role models for others. Muslims are instructed to act piously and to aspire for its highest degree.

Notwithstanding his unsurpassed glory, the Prophet Solomon (peace and blessings be upon him) presented this supplication to Allah, which is marked by humility and surrender to Him:

> *O my Lord! Incline me so that I should be grateful to You for Your favours, which You have bestowed on me and on my parents, and that I should work piously in a way that will please You. And admit me by Your grace to the ranks of Your righteous servants.*
>
> (al-Naml 27:19)

It is a highly desirable act to thank Allah for His numerous favours. Generally speaking, when confronted with a crisis or suffering, one turns to Allah, petitioning relief and comfort. At the same time, one should also remember the countless divine favours enjoyed by oneself and his immediate family, for example, health, resources and happy social relations. This should fill one's heart with gratitude for Allah and should be articulated in the words and good actions one performs. The latter too, represents thanksgiving. The pointed reference to parents in the supplication is for two main reasons: (i) Parents in themselves constitute a major divine favour. For without their care and affection one could not be brought up properly. (ii) Believing parents who impart both the Islamic faith and practices stand out as an invaluable divine gift, for which one should thank Allah profusely. Had Allah not been kind to one's parents in guiding them to sound faith and a pious way of lie, one would have been lost in a life of ignorance, sin and eternal punishment. Furthermore, Allah blessed parents with material resources which, in turn, enabled them to bring their children up decently.

The best way to express thanks to Allah for His numerous favours consists in doing good. Apart from pleasing Allah, it promotes good in society, rendering life pleasant for everyone. For, as is stated in the supplication, being Allah's pious servant is man's highest honour and privilege. The best part though is that this is an attainable honour, open to everyone. It evidently calls for self-discipline and constancy for which one should both strive and invoke Allah's help. Supplicating to Allah is a spiritually rewarding and emotionally soothing exercise. Above all, it is a highly desirable act in Allah's sight, as is evident from the following Qur'ānic passages.

> *And do not covet those things in which Allah has bestowed His gifts more freely on some of you than on others. To men is the portion of what they earn, and to women is the portion of what they earn. And ask Allah of His bounty. For Allah has full knowledge of all things.*
>
> (al-Nisā' 4:32)

> *Ask the forgiveness of Allah, and turn to Him in repentance. For my Lord is always near and ready to answer (supplications).*
>
> (Hūd 11:61)

> *Allah listens to every soul in distress when it calls on Him and relieves its suffering.*
>
> (al-Naml 27:62)

> *Call on your Lord with humility and in private ... call on Him with fear and longing (in your hearts). For the mercy of Allah is always near those who do good.*
>
> (al-A'rāf 7:55-56)

> *When My servants ask you concerning Me, I am indeed close to them. I listen to the prayer of every caller when he calls Me.*
>
> (al-Baqarah 2:186)

The Qur'ān records the supplications of such distinguished persons as

- The Prophet Adam and Eve (al-Baqarah 2:37 and al-A'rāf 7:23)
- The Prophets Abraham and Ishmael (al-Baqarah 2:124 and 126-129)
- Saul's army (al-Baqarah 2:250)
- The believers (al-Baqarah 2:286, Āl 'Imrān 3:8, 9, 16, 26-27, 84, 147, 191-194, al-Mā'idah 5:83, al-Zukhruf 43:13-14, al-Mu'minūn

23:97-98, 109, 118, al-Ḥashr 59:10, al-Furqān 25:74 and al-Aḥqāf 46:15)

- Mary's mother (Āl 'Imrān 3:35)
- The Prophet Zakariyā (Āl 'Imrān 3:38, Maryam 19:5-6 and al-Anbiyā' 21:89)
- The Prophet Jesus (al-Mā'idah 5:114 and 117-118).
- The Prophet Abraham (al-An'ām 6:79, al-Shu'arā' 26:83-89, al-Mumtaḥanah 60:4-5, and Ibrāhīm 14:36-41)
- The Prophet Shu'ayb (al-A'rāf 7:89)
- The Prophet Noah (Hūd 11:47 and Nūḥ 71:28)
- The Prophet Joseph (Yūsuf 12:33-34 and 101)
- The Prophet Muḥammad (al-Isrā' 17:80)
- The Prophet Moses (al-A'rāf 7:149, 151, 156 and 157, Ṭā Hā 20:25-37, al-Shu'arā' 26:12-13 and al-Qaṣaṣ 28:16 and 21-22)
- The Prophet Jonah (al-Anbiyā' 21:87-88)
- The Prophet Job (al-Anbiyā' 21:83)
- The Prophet Solomon (al-Naml 27:19)
- The Queen of Sheba (al-Naml 27:44)

These and many other supplications featured in the Qur'ān are re-echoed in several *aḥādīth.* Not only did the Prophet Muḥammad (peace and blessings be upon him) often make supplications to Allah with the utmost fervour and humility, he also exhorted his Companions to engage in the same. A representative supplication on the Prophet's authority is cited below:

> O my Lord! Keep me firm in my faith. For it is my only defence. Grant me good in the world in which I earn my bread. Improve my prospects in the Next World, to which I have to return ultimately. Make my life a blessing and death as an escape against evil.
>
> (Muslim, *Bāb Faḍl al-Tahlīl wa'l-Du'ā'*)

Needless to add, this takes into account both worlds and seeks their best. As long as one is alive, one should keep on adding good deeds to one's credit and die before one falls prey to some temptation or evil. Both life and death should be thus characterised by good. While the focus is on the Next World, the concerns of this life, especially of one's livelihood, are not neglected. Islam represents the perfect amalgam of both this and that world. A Muslim is not expected to lead an ascetic life, neglecting his obligations towards his parents, wife and children, community and fellow human beings at large. Yet he should not be engrossed in worldly pursuits at the expense of disregarding the Hereafter. The above supplication covers all these points. Some other equally important concerns find mention in the following supplication:

> O our Lord! Infuse mutual love into our hearts and improve our social relations. Guide us to the way of safety and deliver us from darkness into light. Protect us against all indecency and obscenity, both manifest and hidden. Bless our hearing, seeing, hearts, children and wives. Accept our repentance. Surely You are the One to grant pardon. You are Most Merciful. Enable us to thank You for Your bounties. Make us deserving of these and bestow all of these on us.
>
> (*Kanz al-'Ummāl*)

Cordial social relations are essential for a happy, peaceful life for both individuals and society at large. The above underscores the same in invoking Allah for this blessing. Divine guidance is of immense value for man. For it directs him to lead life in the best way and ensures his eternal success in the Next Life. Taking the cue from *Sūrah al-Fātiḥah*, which presses home the same point of being blessed with divine guidance, Allah has bestowed mental and physical faculties on everyone. Likewise, everyone enjoys a family life. However these must be in line with Allah's directive. For example, if the faculties of speech, hearing and sight are abused, these are worse than a curse for man. For their abuse lands man in Hellfire. By the same token, if one deviates from the Sharī'ah code in one's overflowing love for one's wife and children, this too spells eternal damnation. One should, of course, meet their needs and demands. However, resorting to unlawful means to achieve this end amounts to hurling oneself into Hellfire. Accordingly, the above supplication aims at soliciting divine help on this important count. One should make a point of thanking Allah for His numerous favours and turn to Him in sincere repentance for obtaining His forgiveness. Some other relevant points are made in the following supplication which stands out as a testament to the Prophet's sagacity:

> O our Lord! Make us so fearful of You that we shun sin. Make us so obedient to You that we may gain entry into Paradise. Bless us with such conviction that we may bear hardship in this life. Grant us the faculties of hearing and sight and stamina till our last breath. Let our good deeds be a source of good even after our death. Avenge us against the one who oppresses us. Grant us victory over our enemies. Do not make our faith a trial for us. Do not let us devote ourselves wholly to this world, as the goal of all our knowledge and as our destination. Do not impose on us unkind rulers.
>
> (Tirmidhī and Nasā'ī)

It is beyond man's capacity to fear Allah as much as He should be feared. However, at least, one should have such fear of Him as may prevent one from indulging in sin. The same holds true for obedience and surrender to Him. One should come up to the minimum level which entitles one's admission to Paradise. Man is totally dependent on the physical faculties and strength granted to him by Allah. Hence, the plea is for their continuance until one's death. Otherwise, man's life would be utterly miserable and tormenting. Islam does not recommend renunciation of this world, yet it discourages worldliness and material pursuits. A strong note to this effect pervades the above supplication. A few other supplications often recited by the Prophet are reproduced below:

> O our Lord! I seek from You the strength and ability to do good, to shun sin and to help the poor. May You grant me

deliverance and have mercy on me. Make me die before You put me to a test. I seek from You the strength and ability to love You and him who loves You and to prefer such acts which may draw me close to You.

(*Mustadrak* on Thawbān's authority)

O our Lord! I am weak and helpless. Grant me the strength to do all that pleases You. Prompt me to do good enthusiastically. Make Islam my goal. I am humble and disgraced. Grant me honour and glory. I am resourceless. Bless me with sustenance.

(*Mustadrak*, narrated by Baraydah al-Aslamī)

O our Lord! I seek from You the ability to ask of You what suits me most: the best supplication, comprehensive success, abiding reward, and an enviable life record and death.
Keep me steady. Enhance the scale of my good deeds.
Strengthen my faith. Raise my rank. Accept my prayers. I ask of You the highest rank in Paradise.

(*Mustadrak*, narrated by Umm Salamah)

Related Qur'ānic passages for self-study

- al-Baqarah 2:37
- Āl 'Imrān 3:8, 9, 16, 26-27, 84, 147, 191-194
- al-A'rāf 7:23 and 29
- Hūd 11:61
- al-Isrā' 17:110
- Ghāfir 40:14

Reference

1. Daryābādī, *The Glorious Qur'ān*, op. cit., p. 74.

Index